THE GOVERNMENT AND LAW OF GUERNSEY

THE GOVERNMENT AND LAW OF GUERNSEY

Darryl Ogier

with a foreword by the Bailiff of Guernsey

States of Guernsey

2005

© States of Guernsey 2005.

Published in 2005 by The States of Guernsey, Sir Charles Frossard House, La Charroterie, St Peter Port, Guernsey, GY1 1FH. Tel: +44 (0) 1481 717000. Fax: +44 (0) 1481 717299. Website: www.gov.gg.

Typeset by Tradespools, Frome, Somerset, England.

Printed and bound by Antony Rowe Ltd., Chippenham, England.

ISBN:
0-9549775-0-5
978-0-9549775-0-4

Contents

For Harriet, Lucy, and Edward

Foreword

All of us who are involved in the public life of this Bailiwick are regularly asked by strangers to explain how we are governed, and we all have our own thumbnail sketch, which we abridge and expand according to the level of interest of the enquirer. What has not been available is an authoritative and up to date work to which the persistent enquirer interested in learning more may be referred. This comprehensive treatise by Dr Darryl Ogier explains carefully the current composition of and workings of the States of Deliberation, the parish administrations and the various Courts of the Bailiwick. Being a historian Dr Ogier sets the present Constitution in its proper context thus making it easier for readers to understand the reasons for the island's present institutions having evolved in the way that they have.

In addition to looking at the internal workings of the island Dr Ogier has in his final chapters gone on to explain Guernsey's relationship with the outside world, firstly with the government of the United Kingdom and how this has evolved from the more personal relationship that existed with the Crown in earlier times, and secondly through the United Kingdom with the European Community.

The incorporation of the European Convention on Human Rights into the Bailiwick domestic law, the development of the financial services industry and the international requirements for its proper regulation, and the ever increasing treaty obligations of the island in other areas, result in considerable pressures for its institutions to adapt and respond to the demands of the modern world. We are therefore likely to see significant changes in the way that both the States and the Courts conduct themselves over the next ten years, and the accurate recording of what is to be seen at the present time and the helpful historical background will, I am sure, mean that this book will be referred to by future generations as much as it will be by those who are going to benefit from reading it today.

Dr Ogier is to be commended on producing a readable and valuable contribution to the island's historical and legal literature.

de Vic G. Carey
Bailiff of Guernsey
11 November 2004

Les peuples des îles sont plus portés à la liberté que les peuples du continent. Les îles sont ordinairement d'une petite étendue; une partie du peuple ne peut pas être si bien employée à opprimer l'autre; la mer les sépare des grands empires, et la tyrannie ne peut pas s'y prêter la main; les conquérants sont arrêtés par la mer; les insulaires ne sont pas enveloppés dans la conquête, et ils conservent plus aisément leurs lois.

(Islanders enjoy greater freedom than peoples of the Continent do. Islands are generally of a small extent – one part of the people cannot so well be used to oppress the other. The sea separates them from the great empires, and tyranny cannot lend a hand; the sea halts conquerors, the islanders are not swept up in the conquest, and they conserve their laws more easily).

Charles de Secondat,
baron de Montesquieu, (1689–1755),
De l'esprit des lois (1748)
Livre xviii ch. v

Preface

The essay that follows is the work of an historian and citizen of Guernsey, written early in the twenty-first century. Inevitably, it takes a perspective different from existing discussions of the island's government and law, which often have been presented by lawyers, often French or English ones, and often some time ago. (As an historian, I should also add that in the few cases where necessary I have adjusted ancient dates to a modern year, beginning 1 January).[1] Never, in following such a course, has so much been done by so many people for the sake of so few words. It would be invidious to name any here: to all my thanks are sincere. The mistakes and opinions remain my own. I have done my best to state matters as they stood on 24 June 2004.

Darryl Ogier
11 November 2004

---

1.   Until 1752, in Guernsey, as also until then in England, the year officially started 25 March. The 'Act regulating the commencement of the year, and for correcting the calendar now in use' of 1751 (24 Geo. II, c. 23, sometimes known as 'Chesterfield's Act') was registered by Guernsey's Royal Court 28 December 1751.

1. Introduction

Guernsey is one of the Channel Islands. It has an area of about 64 square km, lying in the Bay of St Malo, approximately 50 km west of the Cotentin peninsula of Normandy, 80 km north of Brittany, and some 130 km from the south coast of England. The last official census (2001) found its population to be 59,807. The island and its dependencies Alderney and Sark and some smaller islands (Herm, Brecqhou, Jethou, Burhou, and other islets and reefs) together form the Bailiwick of Guernsey.[1] Jersey, whilst having a similar polity and history, with a few minor dependencies (the rocks and islets of Les Écréhous and Les Minquiers), forms a separate Bailiwick.

The archaeological record strongly suggests Guernsey to have been on prehistoric cross-Channel trade routes.[2] Its town, St Peter Port, was romanised by the second century AD, and possibly before, though what name the Romans knew the port by, if any, is unknown. Celtic missionaries visited the Channel Islands in the early Middle Ages, and later the Vikings were familiar with the archipelago, as attested by the Islands' present names, which are Scandinavian.[3] From 867 the Islands were acknowledged as part of the Breton realm. They had been absorbed into the Norman duchy by the early eleventh century, owing allegiance to its duke.[4]

---

1. The 2001 census recorded the population of Alderney to be 2,294. Sark has a population of approximately 600 persons, and, in 2001, Herm and Jethou (also included in the Guernsey total) had a joint recorded population of 97.

2. Cunliffe, 1986.

3. Coates, 1991 49–54, 118. Guernsey's Gallo-Roman name had been *Lisia*, meaning, perhaps, 'sedge place', or 'place of Liscos', or perhaps neither (Coates, 1991 14–17, 117).

4. The historian Flodoard refers to a grant of 933 of 'the land of the Bretons by the sea' by King Rudolf to William Longsword of Normandy. This has traditionally been understood to include the Channel Islands. However Le Patourel found Flodoard to be 'quite vague', and ' ... if it was decided by the middle of the tenth century that the Channel Islands should not be Breton, it was some time before it could be said with any real meaning that they were Norman ... ': Le Patourel, 1974 440–41, Cf. Le Patourel, 1976 6–8.

1

On William of Normandy's seizure of the English throne in 1066, Guernsey became associated with that realm, although it was to remain part of the Norman duchy. In 1204, King John lost mainland Normandy to the French. Professor Sir James Holt has commented that in the recollection of noteworthy dates '1204 belongs perhaps to a minor calendar', and this is true in English terms.[5] For Guernsey, by contrast, the loss of Normandy recalls an event of fundamental significance in the story of the island and its development. After a period of instability, the Channel Islands were formally recognised under the Treaty of Paris of 1259 to be part of Henry III's continental territories, for which he agreed to do homage. It was, perhaps, only with the coming of the Hundred Years' War, in the thirteen-thirties, that England ceased to regard the Islands as French territories enjoyed by the English Crown.[6]

With its fine roadstead and convenient location between France and England, Guernsey was in the mainstream of commerce between Angevin Gascony and England. Large quantities of wine and other cargoes were shipped through St Peter Port. The island also developed a native industry drying and exporting fish. This trade and the vitality of the island's port were to be the mainstays of Guernsey's economy throughout the later Middle Ages.[7]

A Papal Bull of 1481 directed against attacks on the island had the effect, beneficial to trade, of rendering St Peter Port neutral in times of Anglo-French hostilities. This arrangement survived until 1689.[8] By this time, locally made knitted goods were Guernsey's major export, although the wine business remained important. In the sixteenth and seventeenth centuries trade between Guernsey's Calvinist merchants and their co-religionists in France and elsewhere was lively.[9] Although the island suffered during the mid sixteen-hundreds, not least because Castle Cornet (just off St Peter Port) differed with the island in the Civil War, the late seventeenth century saw a recovery, with Guernsey developing as a significant *entrepôt* in the Atlantic economy.[10] Generally, although the island was again on the frontier, the eighteenth century was prosperous,

---

5. Holt, 1975 223.
6. Stevenson, 1975; Le Patourel, 1962 201–02.
7. Williams, 1928.
8. Jacqueline, 1978, and p. 87, below.
9. Ogier, 1996 173–77.
10. Stevens Cox, 1999.

seeing much commercial and other activity in the era of the Revolutionary and Napoleonic Wars.

In some respects, Guernsey experienced the general depression following those Wars, yet the islanders were able to find and pursue new enterprises.[11] The export of large quantities of stone commenced in the early nineteenth century. The coming of the Age of Steam opened English and other markets to Guernsey produce, such as cattle, grapes, flowers, and tomatoes. The period also witnessed a steepening in the decline of the use of the French language in official matters and of the Norman-French *patois* by the wider population. The export of horticultural crops continued through much of the twentieth century, although interrupted by enemy occupation 1940–45.[12] Faster communications also facilitated the development of Guernsey as a tourist destination. These two aspects of island business remain important today, although the provision of financial services, centred in St Peter Port, now predominates economically.

---

11. Duncan, 1841 261–62; Tupper, 1876 505–06.
12. Cruickshank, 1975; Bell, 2002.

2. Parish Administration

The Douzaines

Guernsey's ten ancient ecclesiastical parishes form the island's present day civil administrative districts, and the seven States' electoral districts follow parish boundaries, save for that purpose St Peter Port is split into two.[1] The main parochial bodies are the *Douzaines*. As their name suggests, they usually have twelve members, known as *Douzeniers*, although the parish of the Vale has sixteen,[2] and that of St Peter Port, twenty. Under *The Reform (Guernsey) Law*, 1948, as amended, Douzeniers are elected by persons inscribed on the respective parishes' electoral rolls, serving a term of office of six years, at the expiration of which they are eligible for re-election.[3] The title 'Dean of the Douzaine' is usually assumed by the longest serving Douzenier, although sometimes, even if on no statutory basis, a Douzaine will elect a Douzenier as Dean.[4] The Deans of the Douzaines until recently had responsibilities relating to the elections of Constables, and still serve on the panel

---

1. Which parish is in which electoral district is set out below, at p. 23.

2. An Act of the Royal Court of 10 December 1614 united the Douzaines of the two districts of the Vale, namely of the *Clos du Valle* (apparently served by twelve Douzeniers) and the *Vingtaine de l'Épine* (apparently served by four) stating that the parish should be served by no more than a total of twelve Douzeniers, with four to be elected from the *Vingtaine* in place of four of those from the *Clos*, as vacancies through death arose. This appears not to have been implemented, and a united Douzaine of sixteen to have been the permanent result. The manuscript in Guernsey's Greffe from which 'Warburton', 1822 was printed suggests that in the seventeenth century the numbers of Douzeniers sometimes varied in other parishes also, for sound administrative reasons, although this passage does not occur in the printed edition (on both of which see Clark, 1984 and Ogier, 1990 i).

3. By States' resolution of 27 November 2002 elections of Douzeniers, and to the other parish offices treated in this chapter, are normally to be held throughout Guernsey on the first Wednesday in November annually, so abolishing the duty of Deans of the Douzaines under Article 54 of *The Reform (Guernsey) Law*, 1948, as amended, to fix the dates for the election of Parish Constables. The legislation providing for this is in preparation.

4. The junior Douzenier is sometimes known, in Guernsey-French, as *le foulleau*, ie. 'the runt'. This is not a creature of statute either.

constituting Administrative Decision Review Boards (though these are set for abolition, as will be explained in Chapter four).

The early history of the Douzaines is not known, although they may have originated as parish juries of presentment, which delivered opinions to medieval assizes. On the other hand, they may have been pre-existing bodies, which took on such a responsibility.[5] Their duties traditionally included the regulation of boundaries and the repair of roads, the apportionment of parishioners' liability for taxes and supervision of their collection by the now obsolete officers known as *Vingteniers*, and participation in the division of the real estates lying in their parishes of deceased persons.[6]

The parishes' executive officers are the two Parish Constables. Historically they had police functions, making criminal investigations and supervising strangers. They also took the opinions of parishioners in

---

5. Evidence presented to the justices of assize in the late thirteenth and early fourteenth centuries had been given by parish juries of presentment, who were required to 'come by twelve', (Havet, 1878 117, n.3). Similarly in 1274 and 1331, when *extentes* of royal revenues were compiled, the evidence of twelve jurors from each parish commonly was taken (Société Jersiaise, 1877; de Sausmarez, 1934). *Circa* 1309, juries present at the assizes (in Jersey) were referred to as '*duzeynes*', (Le Patourel, 1937 58, n.9), but whether these juries were parish douzaines, or their predecessors, or something quite separate and impermanent, cannot really be said. There is that coincidence of twelve worthies representing their parishes, and some sort of parochial administration must have been necessary in the middle ages.

6. 'Warburton', 1822 63–65. Douzaines whose parishes are prevailingly upon the fiefs of St Michel and Le Roi once had the additional obligation periodically to compose the manorial surveys known as *livres de perchage*, ie. 'books of measurement'. The Douzaines were also involved in the allotment of the *vingtième* and *préciput*. The former of these (abolished in the town in 1566, and elsewhere in 1840) was the entitlement of all sons between them to a one-twentieth share in the deceased's estate. It was worked out by the sons in the presence of the Douzaine and tended to incorporate the most valuable parts of the estate. It could be levied only in circumstances where the number of daughters was no more than twice the number of sons. The Douzaine out of the *vingtième* allotted the *préciput* to the eldest son as his birthright. Once he indicated his choice the land was measured and evaluated by the Douzaine, with no regard to buildings etc., standing on it, to see that he had his entitlement. The *Loi sur les Successions*, 1840, limited the area of the *préciput*, and restricted it to the main *enclos* of the house etc., save where its area was less than one-third of all the land to be divided, in which case the eldest son could demand up to one-third of the whole estate, in addition to the *préciput*, on providing compensation to his co-heirs in respect of the surplus award. On this see Jeremie, 1866 34–50. *Préciputs* were abolished under *The Law of Inheritance*, 1954, although these have, though increasingly rarely, still been levied in recent years in respect of the estates of people dying before the coming into force of the law of 1954.

elections to the Royal Court, received taxes for transmission to the States, and regulated highways, bakeries, and taverns.[7] Before the coming into force in 1844 of an Order in Council reforming the assembly, the Constables of each parish (usually one in the eighteenth and nineteenth centuries,[8] seemingly both in the earlier period) represented their respective Douzaines in the States of Deliberation, as they had done for three hundred years, and probably longer.[9] Parishioners elect Constables for terms of three years, although outside St Peter Port they generally serve for only two, in order to facilitate an easy succession.[10]

An Ordinance of 23 October 1676 required the Douzeniers of St Peter Port to have first served as Parish Constable. This requirement was abolished by the *Loi relative à la Douzaine de la Ville et Paroisse de Saint Pierre Port*, 1900, and now the opposite is usually the case, with one or another of the town's Douzeniers seeking election as Constable. In the other parishes, Constables often aspire to what there is regarded as the more senior position. This is, one supposes, an outcome of the differences that have developed in the respective duties and authority of the offices in town and country, and also the fact that, as just noted, after the mid nineteenth century the Constables ceased automatically representing their parishes in the States of Deliberation, being replaced by Douzaine representatives. Article 73 of the Reform Law of 1948 prohibited any Advocate of the Royal Court from serving as a Parish Constable, a situation arising as a consequence of the Constables' one-time police functions, even though these had disappeared under the *Loi ayant rapport à la Police Salariée pour l'Ile entière*, 1920. This prohibition was removed by *The Reform (Guernsey) (Amendment) Law*, 2003.

---

7. Ogier, 1996 15–16.
8. Hocart, 1988 4.
9. Ogier, 1990 ii.
10. An Ordinance of the Royal Court of 5 October 1778 stated that the office was annual, but that elections might be held three-yearly, though not after a longer period.

Parish business

The senior Constable normally presides at Douzaine meetings, which generally are convened monthly. The Constables keep records such as minutes and accounts, publish announcements, bring *Billets d'État* (agendas and associated material) for States' meetings to the notice of the parish, and supervise elections of Douzeniers, under Article 54 of *The Reform (Guernsey) Law*, 1948, as amended. The Constables' and Douzaines' responsibilities extend to the supervision of polls at general and parochial elections, granting permits to build near highways (*permis*),[11] issuing dog licences, and ensuring that hedges are cut. They organise the collection of rubbish, and the administration of parish cemeteries, and give permission for events such as the opening of shops on Sundays, as provided for under *The Sunday Trading Ordinance*, 2002.[12] The Constables and Douzaines play roles in ensuring public safety in regard to buildings, cisterns, construction sites and road works, and regulate the erection of scaffolding. They also see that quarries are properly fenced, reporting on defaulters to the Royal Court's Michaelmas session of Chief Pleas. They are directed by legislation to report in matters of the licensing by the Royal Court and other bodies of auctioneers, those selling liquor, and the establishment of betting shops, public halls (*salles publiques*), steam engines, and (in the town) bakers' ovens. Musicians performing in the streets of St Peter Port require parish permission, and that parish also controls the keeping of pigs, if any, in certain districts.[13]

The Douzaines levy an Occupiers' Rate, under the *Loi relative à la Taxation Paroissiale*, 1923. This provides for taxation for necessities

---

11.   These are colloquially referred to as *bornements*, though these latter historically related to the adjustment and amendment of boundaries, especially with regard to roads: Duncan, 1841 498, says 'in the formation of streets or roads within the parish, the Douzaine fix the boundaries, or give, what is locally termed, *les bornemens*'. Cf. 'Warburton', 1822 64. The first Ordinance of the Royal Court on the subject, which may reflect earlier practice, is one of 6 October 1628. It was reiterated by one of 18 April 1726, which also instructs the Constables and Douzaines to undertake annual inspections of hedges bounding highways. *Bornements* are presently the subject of an Ordinance dated 25 April 1931 (made permanent 1948), as amended.

12.   The Ordinance is due to be amended, though not as respects the role of the parish authorities, following a States' resolution of 1 August 2003.

13.   Jehan, 1983. Most parishes also have committees, which are not of the Douzaine, to deal with interests such as concern cemeteries, street lighting and moorings.

including the ecclesiastical needs detailed in the next chapter, the costs of parochial administration, and other public necessities as various as the maintenance of street furniture, including lighting, the making of contributions to parish school libraries, etc.[14] Collection of Occupiers' Rate follows an annual meeting of ratepayers and the approval by the Royal Court of a subsequent application, or *remède*. A separate *remède* is required to collect a refuse rate, dedicated to rubbish collection, which is the subject of *The Parochial Collection of Refuse (Guernsey) Law*, 2001, as amended. Both are assessed according to the rateable values of properties, set by the States' *Cadastre*.

Although the Social Security Department of the States, as successor to the Guernsey Social Security Authority, generally provides island-wide social security coverage, through social and health insurance, and other schemes,[15] each parish elects annually two Procureurs of the Poor to serve two-year offices in junior and senior positions, save in St Peter Port, where six Overseers of the Poor are similarly appointed. These, in liaison with the States' Social Security Department and Parochial Outdoor Assistance Boards,[16] provide from States' sources, under the *Public Assistance Law*, 1937, as amended, emergency support to those unable to meet basic standards of living. In St Peter Port, a single Procureur of the Poor also distributes monies, from a separate and ancient parish charitable fund, which is not subject to the Public Assistance Law, in order to meet urgent want.

The Douzaines and the States of Guernsey

Until the year 2004, each Douzaine appointed a Douzaine Representative to serve as its member in the States of Deliberation. Douzeniers and Constables were equally eligible for appointment, and individuals often served several periods of office. Whilst presenting the views of their Douzaines in debate, Representatives voted as their consciences dictated, as allowed for by Article 16 of the 1948 Reform Law. The States, by resolution of 27 November 2002, voted to abolish the position from 1

---

14. For the earlier period, see van Leuven, 1997 111–16.
15. Under *The Social Insurance (Guernsey) Law*, 1978 (wherein the Department is designated 'The States Insurance Authority').
16. Though elected by the States, these are non-governmental bodies, constituted by Article 5 of *The Public Assistance (Guernsey) Amendment Law*, 1957.

May 2004, and this was effected under *The Reform (Guernsey) (Amendment) Law*, 2003. The Douzaines are still represented in the States of Election, an electoral college which appoints Jurats, as provided for under Article 16 of the 1948 Reform Law, amended by *The Reform (Guernsey) (Amendment) Law*, 2003, whereunder no Douzenier (or People's Deputy) is allowed concurrently to be a Jurat, and vice-versa.

3. The Church

The origin of the ancient ecclesiastical parishes is unclear, although six of their churches are attested from the 1050s and the others from a century later.[1] The nineteenth century saw the creation of the ecclesiastical districts of St John, Holy Trinity, St Stephen, and St James (this last now defunct) to serve particular communities within the existing parish of St Peter Port, and that of St Matthew, within the parish of Ste Marie du Castel. These differ in status from the ancient parishes – which, as seen in the previous chapter, form the fundamental administrative units – and are not treated further here.

The Norman regime

In the Middle Ages, just as the Channel Islands were in Normandy's administrative system, so they were part of the Duchy's church, being parts of the Diocese of Coutances, apparently in the twelfth century in their own archdeaconry *de insulis*, and later being absorbed into the archdeaconry of Bauptois.[2] From the eleventh century, the Bishop of Coutances and various religious houses had extensive interests in the Islands' parishes and their churches. In Guernsey, the abbot of Mont St Michel enjoyed four advowsons (the right to appoint parsons to the churches) and the others belonged to the abbot of Marmoutier (Touraine). One of the latter later came into the gift of the abbot of Blanchelande (Manche). The Bishop of Coutances enjoyed those of Sark and Alderney. The Abbey of Notre Dame de Voeu at Cherbourg had Herm, and Mont St Michel, Jethou. The possession by French religious houses and ecclesiastics of fiefs, land and other rights and revenues throughout the Islands necessitated the establishment of dative priories, and there were probably thirteen of them in 1204.[3]

---

1. Fauroux, 1961 no. 141; Round, 1899 no. 736.
2. De Gruchy, 1957 94; Le Patourel, 1937 32.
3. Stevenson, 1975 237. It might be questioned whether this 'dative' function has not been stressed at the expense of the spiritual. Note, for example, that the priory of

The rights and properties of the Bishop and the French religious houses (the so called 'alien priories') were regularly taken 'into the king's hand' in times of war. At an indeterminate point, probably in the late fourteenth century, the confiscation became permanent. The English Crown (or, occasionally, secular magnates enjoying the island's revenues under it) thereafter made appointments to ecclesiastical livings and enjoyed what once had been the property of the alien priories.[4] Notwithstanding this secularisation, the Bishop of Coutances continued to induct priests and rectors, and the Channel Islands remained in the Norman diocese.[5]

The Winchester connection

It was the Reformation that finally separated Guernsey from the Diocese of Coutances. By a letter of June 1568, referring to a Papal Bull of 1500 (the authenticity of which is doubtful)[6] Elizabeth I notified the

---

St Michel de la Royfrarie not only administered the small fief – now known as 'La Rue Frairie' – of its motherhouse, the Abbey of St Leufroi, in Guernsey, but also, as its name suggests, was a Royal chantry: de Guerin, 1909 i 81–82, and cf. Le Patourel, 1982 *passim*.

4. Le Patourel, 1982 111–12.

5. Lee, 1889.

6. On 28 October 1496, Henry VII had obtained a Bull from Pope Alexander VI transferring the Channel Islands from the jurisdiction of Coutances to the Diocese of Salisbury, noting that disputes between the French and English meant that the Coutances' interest could be detrimental to the islanders, and therefore subjecting them to an English bishop. This Bull is genuine, and to be found enrolled on the Papal registers. The Bishop of Salisbury at the time it was made was John Blythe. He died 23 August 1499, and his successor, Henry Deane, was not appointed, provisionally, until 8 January 1500. He was restored in the temporalities of the see on 22 March 1500, but appears not to have been consecrated before he was translated to Canterbury 26 May 1501. In the meantime, a purported further Papal Bull, dated 20 January 1500, had appeared. This ostensibly cancelled the transfer to Salisbury, and instead placed the Channel Islands under the authority of Thomas Langton, Bishop of Winchester. In a letter to Langton, who was soon to be selected as Archbishop of Canterbury, the king explained that notwithstanding the Salisbury aspect, '... considering afterward that the said isles be next adjoining to the coast of this our realm where your jurisdiction lieth, thought it therefore most convenient that you should have the pastoral cure of them before any other ...', therefore desiring the Bishop to 'take upon you the spiritual care and ordinary charge of our said isles and to constitute and send thither your officers sufficient as well for the execution of the same Bull as for the exercising of the spiritual jurisdiction committed to you in that behalf' (Lee, 1904 256). Perhaps, besides his geographical motive, the king had also thought to favour Langton, which could conveniently be done at this

inhabitants of Guernsey that she 'annexed and united' the Channel Islands to the Bishops of Winchester, who were 'to govern and direct Our ecclesiastical estate in the said Isles'. An Order in Council of 11 March 1569 confirmed that the Queen's letter 'perpetually united' the Islands to the Diocese of Winchester, and that the Bishop was constituted Ordinary of them, going on to confirm, in a manner reminiscent of confirmations in respect of secular legal procedures, made about the same time, that the Dean of Guernsey might not 'compel any of the inhabitants of the said isle to repair into England for any ecclesiastical cause, but that the same may be determined there by commission, unless it be by the assent of both parties according to the ancient usages of the said isle'.[7] The Queen, represented by the Lieutenant-Governor, still presents Guernsey's Rectors and Dean for induction by the Bishop of Winchester.[8]

The Dean of Guernsey

The office of Dean of Guernsey is first mentioned in 1295, in the English Close Rolls, where the name of one Nicolas Meriene occurs,

---

time, when Salisbury was between bishops. The Bull of 1500 was registered at Winchester. No trace of it appears, however, on the registers of Coutances, and – still more significantly – on those of the Vatican. One cannot but regard it as unofficial, to say the least. Bishop Langton is known to have made a single appointment of a Channel Island priest: to Jersey on 1 January 1501 (Lee, 1904 257), before his translation to Canterbury a few weeks later. Langton had died by the end of that month. Under Langton's successor, Richard Fox, the Bishop of Coutances – and by implication Guernsey's Deanery and churches – continued as if neither Bull, of 1496 and 1500, whether genuine or spurious, had ever existed. Even the Jersey priest who was preferred to St Brelade's by Langton, was similarly appointed by the Bishop of Coutances within weeks of the first action, and 1497 had seen a visit to the Islands by the Bishop of Coutances' suffragan. Nothing more of Guernsey's attachment to Winchester was heard for a considerable time, and indeed in 1550 the English Privy Council endorsed the Bishop of Coutances' right to receive his Channel Island revenues (Eagleston, 1949 50).

7. Lee, 1904 263–65. On secular similarities see pp. 59–60, 86–88, 108–09, below.

8. In spite of what has sometimes been said, this does not mean that the parishes are 'Royal Peculiars', according to the usual definition of those things, for which see Barber, 1995. A further argument has sometimes been advanced that the Archbishop of Canterbury's legatine powers do not extend to the Bailiwick because the islands were in a foreign Archdiocese (that of Rouen) at the time of The Ecclesiastical Licences Act 1534. That Act however extended to all Henry VIII's dominions, and there seems no reason not to think that it included, if awkwardly, the Channel Island churches.

but, by analogy with Jersey, there is good reason to suppose it existed by the late eleventh century.[9] The Dean is usually the incumbent of an island parish, though eighteenth-century precedent suggests that this is not a requirement.[10] The Dean presently is *ex officio* a Canon of Winchester Cathedral, President of the Deanery Synod and the Deanery Standing Committee, an *ex officio* member of the Diocesan Standing Committee, Joint President of the Guernsey Council of Churches, chairman of the Elizabeth College Board of Directors,[11] and a member of the Priaulx Library Council.[12] The Dean of either of the Channel Island Bailiwicks is, by arrangement between them, also a member of the General Synod of the Church of England.

The Ecclesiastical Court

In the Medieval period problems with islanders bringing local cases before the Bishop's Court at Coutances and elsewhere led to the delegation of a certain jurisdiction establishing Guernsey's Ecclesiastical Court. The Dean of the island was made a Special Commissary of the Bishop in order to exercise this jurisdiction.[13] Today, the Dean of Guernsey usually still presides in the Ecclesiastical Court as Commissary, although historically there have been occasions when the offices have not conjoined in the same individual.[14] The Rectors of the island parishes may assist in the Court as assessors (priests-in-charge seem not, in this context, to be regarded as occupying the equivalent position, although they do in most other respects following the implementation of *The Priests-in-Charge (Assimilation to Rectors) (Guernsey) Law*, 1999). The Court is organised by its Registrar, and its executive officer is an

9. Stapleton, 1840–44 I 26.
10. Duncan, 1841 351.
11. Constituted by an Order in Council registered 11 January 1853, as amended.
12. Constituted under an agreement approved by the States 30 July 1880. The Dean formerly sat on the States' Ecclesiastical and Liberation Religious Service Committees, the duties of which have been subsumed in those of the Legislation Select Committee and Culture and Leisure Department respectively.
13. Le Patourel, 1937 33.
14. Carey, 1889 17.

apparitor.[15] In contentious matters, pleadings are heard from proctors, who in practice are sworn in from amongst the Advocates of the Royal Court. The Law Officers of the Crown are *ex officio* Her Majesty's Proctors in the Court. The Court last convened in full session, and perhaps even then *ultra vires*, in 1952.[16]

In the fifteenth and sixteenth centuries, Guernsey's secular powers were not reluctant to regulate the activities of the religious.[17] The Ecclesiastical Court ceased to operate at the Reformation and an alternative Presbyterian régime prevailed for a century. In 1662, the Court was revived and Anglicanism enforced. The Court's responsibilities included now abrogated functions such as regulating matrimonial affairs, education, abjurations by Roman Catholics, the administration of other oaths, etc., and the matters that are still within its jurisdiction: the granting, in respect of personal estates, of probate and, in intestacies, letters of administration, the issue of faculties for building works, disposals of or additions to church ornament, and exhumations, marriage licences, and the sequestration of vacant benefices.[18] It also swears in notaries public and churchwardens.

The Ecclesiastical Court's jurisdiction in matrimonial causes, save in respect of granting marriage licences, was transferred to the Royal Court under the *Loi sur Empêchements au Mariage à cause de Parenté, et sur l'Etablissement de la Juridiction Civile dans les Causes Matrimoniales, 1939. The Ecclesiastical Court (Jurisdiction) (Bailiwick of Guernsey) Law*, 1994 limited the probate jurisdiction of the Court to the granting of probate and issuing of letters of administration in respect of the personal estates of deceased persons, denying the Court any purported role in settling disputes in such areas, save as the Royal Court may direct.[19] The Royal Court also directs the Ecclesiastical Court with regard to grants of probate and the issue of letters of administration in cases where a *caveat* is lodged. The Ecclesiastical Court does retain the power to make decisions in respect of contentious faculty applications. Usually the

---

15. 'An officer appointed by an ecclesiastical judge to execute the orders and decrees of his court, and to summon persons to appear before it (hence the name)': Cross and Livingstone, 1997 92. Presumably H.M. Sergeant's office would be asked to supply an officer to serve in such a capacity should the Court have the need.
16. Ozanne, 1993 108–09.
17. De Guérin, 1914 158–62; Ogier, 1996 11, 21–22.
18. Ozanne, 1993 108.
19. Cf. Carey, 1889 21.

Commissary will sit alone on such matters, although he does have power to convene a full court if he considers this necessary.[20]

The upkeep of the churches

Church buildings in the Medieval period were maintained from the regular and accumulated gifts of the faithful, particularly in *rentes*, and also, in some degree, from the resources of their monastic patrons, though the latter had dropped out of the picture by the early fifteenth century. For of a variety of reasons, the relevant parochial funds – the *trésors et fabriques* – became severely depleted at the Reformation, so much so that by the time of the Restoration and imposition of Anglicanism the churches were in a dilapidated state. Following representations made by the Dean of Guernsey, on 24 March 1677 a royal letter, eliding any responsibility that might have been alleged against the Crown as successor to the alien priory patrons, instructed that churchwardens, after certain formalities, might in cases of necessity apply to the Royal Court to raise assessed amounts 'as they have heretofore used in the like case'. This apparently referred to an existing *ad hoc* tax on parishioners, which was to continue. As stated in a petition of 1816, 'For the repairs of parochial churches a separate revenue under the name of "trésor" is appropriated to each of them, and if not sufficient a rate or tax is levied on the parishioners according to their respective incomes …'.[21] In 1868, a *Loi relative à la Taxation Paroissiale* regularised the regime under which the ratepayers are responsible for the payment of an ecclesiastical rate for the upkeep of church property.

The ecclesiastical rate is raised as part of the annual parish Occupiers' Rate, and is today governed by the *Loi relative à la Taxation Paroissiale*, 1923, as amended. It provides for such things as repairs to the parish church and churchyard, the structure of and exterior of the rectory, insurance, one-half of the costs of cleaning, payment of bell-ringers, provision of church registers etc. An annual meeting, usually held in the spring, convened by the Rector and Churchwardens, approves the raising of funds, as provided for in the *Loi relative aux Assemblées Paroissiales*, 1902. For practical reasons, this meeting usually precedes that held for the raising of the secular part of the Occupiers' Rate, and

---

20. Ozanne, 2002.
21. Carey, 1925 36.

indeed it is the Parish Constables who approach the Royal Court for a *remède* to levy sums voted. The ecclesiastical meeting also approves the Churchwardens' accounts (under an Ordinance of 18 May 1809), witnesses the Dean or his delegate approving the audited accounts of the *trésor*, elects the People's Warden, and hears the Rector nominate his Warden.[22]

The Churchwardens

The Churchwardens are recorded under various titles from Medieval times: the Ordinance of 1809 calls them *Curateurs des Trésors*, and this is what they remain. With the Rector, these two officers, one designated the People's Warden, the other the Rector's, control church property. The Churchwardens are responsible to the Bishop of Winchester's Commissary annually to supply answers to questions concerning the physical state of the parish church, rectory, insurance etc. They may also refer to such other things they deem worth reporting, including matters relating to the incumbent. The Churchwardens are responsible for obtaining faculties from the Ecclesiastical Court for works to Church property, for the *trésors* and other funds held in trust by the Church, for good order during Divine service, and for providing the registers and certificates usual and necessary to parish life.

Under the Ordinance of 1809, once elected, Churchwardens cannot be compelled to serve for more than a year in office, nor – like the Parish Constables – may they serve for more than three years without a further election taking place. Both should be resident in the parish, although if a Rector's Warden cannot be found, it is permissible to appoint a person from outside, with the parish Douzaine's agreement, and after application to the Ecclesiastical Court. The Ecclesiastical Court swears in all Churchwardens, and they have to apply to the same body should they seek to resign.[23]

---

22. Robilliard, 1998 7–14. The Royal Court confirmed the Rector's right to appoint his nominee by its judgment of 15 January 1828, in a case between the Rector of St Peter Port and his parishioners: Jacob, 1830 254–55.
23. Robilliard, 1998.

Church Measures and the General Synod of the Church of England

The United Kingdom's Church of England Assembly (Powers) Act 1919 transferred from Parliament to a newly-created National Assembly of the Church of England ('the Church Assembly') the power to legislate in church matters, other than those of a theological or doctrinal nature, by Measures presented by the Assembly to Parliament for approval before receiving Royal Assent. Matters of Canon Law remained the responsibility of the clerical Convocations of Canterbury and York, which submitted their resolutions directly to the Crown for assent. The Synodical Government Measure 1969 transferred many of the powers of both the Church Assembly and the Convocations to the newly created General Synod of the Church of England.

Measures of the Church Assembly made in its early years did not extend to Guernsey. Their terms were not automatically compatible with the island's constitution, nor was the Bailiwick represented in the Assembly. The situation was regularised by an Order in Council of 26 October 1931. This conveyed The Channel Islands (Representation) Measure 1931 and The Channel Islands (Church Legislation) Measure 1931 to the Royal Court for registration. The Synodical Government Measure 1969 was extended under the Synodical Government (Channel Islands) Order 1970, registered in Guernsey on 25 August 1970. Taken together, these Measures (as amended)[24] effectively provide for the application of Church Measures in the Bailiwick, island representation in the General Synod (formerly the Church Assembly) and the Synod of the Diocese of Winchester (formerly the Diocesan Conference). When a Measure is to be extended, wholly or in part, the procedure requires the preparation of a scheme by the Bishop in consultation with the Guernsey Deanery Synod, comprising beneficed and licensed clergy, and lay representatives elected by the sixteen congregations in the Deanery. The draft scheme is transmitted to the United Kingdom Government's Department for Constitutional Affairs, which conveys it via the Bailiff's Office to the States' Legislation Select Committee. The Legislation Select Committee, after consultation with the Standing Committee of the Guernsey Deanery Synod, thereupon reports on it to

---

24. By The Channel Islands (Church Legislation) Measure, 1931 (Amendment) Measure, 1957, registered by the Royal Court 28 June 1958.

the States. If the States approve the scheme, it then goes before the General Synod of the Church of England for approval or rejection. On approval, any scheme is then returned to the Department for Constitutional Affairs, from where it is transmitted to the Privy Council, which embodies the scheme in an Order in Council, for registration in Guernsey in the usual manner, as described in the next chapter.

The ecclesiastical law

Guernsey's ecclesiastical law cannot be said with certainty to correspond with that of England. An Order in Council of 15 July 1662 addressed to the island's authorities effectively embodied the Act of Uniformity's provisions concerning the Book of Common Prayer. By Dr Jean de Sausmarez's commission as Dean of Guernsey of 14 July 1664 (annexed to an Order in Council registered in Guernsey on 19 August 1665) the Dean's jurisdiction was limited to within the bounds established by the English Canons drawn up by Convocation in 1603 and approved by the Crown in 1604. Although these Canons appear often to have been regarded as persuasive in the island, none were specifically promulged for Guernsey. About 1700, some attempt was made to regularise affairs, either by formally adopting the Canons of 1604 or those for Jersey of 1623, but the matter appears not to have been resolved.[25] It remains the case that there are no specific Canons for Guernsey, although the Jersey Canons have been under review for quite some time,[26] and it may one day happen that the Bailiwick of Guernsey will adopt these, in a revised form.

Hence, although the English Act of Supremacy of 1559 expressed itself as applying within 'this realm or within any other your Majesty's dominions or countries ...', and the Act of Uniformity of the same year extended to England, Wales, 'or other the Queen's dominions',[27] it was to be more than a century before Guernsey was brought near to the Church of England. The organisation of the local church today still differs from that in England, not only in the operation of the Ecclesiastical Court, but also with regard to the

25. Lawrence, 1926 21–32.
26. Hibbs, 1998 261–62.
27. Tanner, 1930 130–35.

means of upkeep of the ancient parish churches, and the duties of Churchwardens in connection with them. The manner of the extension of ecclesiastical legislation to Guernsey and the island's ecclesiastical law are similarly distinctive.

4. The States of Guernsey

The assembly of the Royal Court, Clergy and Parish Constables that historically formed the States possibly existed in some form in the fifteenth century, and perhaps earlier, since elections by Guernsey's *habitans et demouranz* (inhabitants and residents) are referred to in the *Précepte d'Assize* of 1441, which purports to be a statement of fourteenth-century practice. The assembly is first recorded by name, in its French form, (*les États*) in 1538.[1] This body was the direct precursor of the modern States of Deliberation, Guernsey's parliamentary assembly. Why States' assemblies first convened is uncertain, and although Guernsey's Royal Court maintained the legislative upper hand until the mid nineteenth century, it may be the case that meetings came to be summoned not only with the elective function described below, but also in order that the Court might gauge the views of the wider population, concerning other matters of common concern. Another possibility is that the States developed out of the Court of Chief Pleas, as may also have happened in Alderney.[2] Neither explanation is certain, nor exclusive of the other.

In the sixteenth century, the States met as the need arose, most often to elect Jurats of the Royal Court and the Court's executive officer known as the *Prévôt*. After a period of desuetude, the States were re-established in 1605, and, whilst power remained concentrated in the Royal Court, they assumed a greater role in government for the next few decades. By the eighteenth century, however, members met irregularly, with functions limited to dealing with military affairs, raising taxes, addressing the Crown on behalf of the people when this was thought necessary, maintaining Elizabeth College and St Peter Port harbour, and controlling the sale of corn in times of want.[3] Richard Hocart has dealt authoritatively with the States' subsequent development up to the

---

1. Ogier, 1990 ii 44; Eagleston, 1924.
2. Cf. Commission 1846, 1848 195–96; van Leuven, 2004 134–35.
3. Hocart, 1988 4–5.

constitutional reforms of 1948, and therefore this is not treated in detail here.[4]

The States of Election

A Royal Commission of 1607 identified a body of 'the Bailiff and Jurats, with the Constables and Dozens of every parish' to elect the Jurats of the Royal Court and the *Prévôt*.[5] Sir Peter Stafford Carey (1803–86, Bailiff 1845–83) argued before the Royal Commission appointed in 1846 that this merely referred to the States in their fullest form.[6] Even so, by the 1770s this greater assembly – which by then also included the incumbents of the ancient parishes – was distinctly known as the States *of Election*.[7] In 1844, the States of Election's responsibilities were widened, making the levy of some island-wide taxes subject to their approval, and between 1948 and 1993 the assembly was the vehicle for the election of *Conseillers*.

Taxation no longer forms any part of the States of Election's business, and following reforms relating to the manner of appointment of H.M. Sheriff (as the Prévôt is now known) and States' Conseillers, treated below, they currently form solely an electoral college to elect the Jurats, meeting when necessary, usually immediately before a meeting of the States of Deliberation. Before 1948, the States of Election comprised the Bailiff and Jurats of the Royal Court and their fellow members of the States of Deliberation (as the other limb had come to be known) together with the junior Constables and all the parishes' Douzeniers. The assembly today comprises:

The Bailiff
The Jurats
The Rectors or Priests-in-Charge (subject to the provisions of *The Reform (Amendment) (Guernsey) Law*, 1984, which requires any to have been resident in Guernsey for twelve months or more)
H.M. Procureur
H.M. Comptroller
The People's Deputies of the States of Deliberation, and

---

4. Hocart, 1988.
5. Commission 1607, 1814 46.
6. Commission 1846, 1848 116.
7. Hocart, 1988 3.

thirty-four Douzaine Representatives elected for each meeting of the States of Election by their respective Douzaines, as follows:

Saint Peter Port, nine Douzeniers
Saint Sampson, five Douzeniers
Vale, five Douzeniers
Castel, five Douzeniers
Saint Saviour, two Douzeniers
Saint Pierre du Bois, one Douzenier
Torteval, one Douzenier
Forest, one Douzenier
Saint Martin, four Douzeniers, and
Saint Andrew, one Douzenier

The Reform (Guernsey) (Amendment) Law, 2003, provides that the States of Deliberation may vary by resolution the allocation of the numbers of Douzaine Representatives, so as to reflect the sizes of the populations of the parishes, though the total must remain thirty-four. The same Law also provides that a Douzaine Representative is not obliged to vote according to the instructions of the Douzaine, but according to his or her own preference.

The States of Deliberation

The States of Deliberation is a parliamentary assembly acting by and through its Departments and Committees (and in this study, unless the contrary is made clear, it is to the States of Deliberation that the words 'the States' refer). The assembly is constituted under *The Reform (Guernsey) Law*, 1948 as amended, most significantly recently by *The Reform (Guernsey) (Amendment) Law*, 2003. The States of Deliberation presently comprise a Presiding Officer, who is *ex officio* the Bailiff, or in his absence the Deputy Bailiff, serving as Deputy Presiding Officer, or an Acting Presiding Officer nominated from the members by the Bailiff. Each serves as a moderator, and exercises neither an original nor casting vote.[8] The members are the Law Officers of the Crown (H.M. Procureur

---

8.   Under the Reform Law of 1948, the Bailiff or his substitute had a casting vote, but now, under Article 1(4) of *The Reform (Guernsey) (Amendment) Law*, 2003, he has 'no casting vote, and in the event of an equality of votes he shall (except in the case of an election) declare the proposition lost'.

and H.M. Comptroller) who may not vote, and by convention only address the assembly when answering questions or offering legal advice on matters under debate, and speaking on constitutional and related matters, two representatives of the States of Alderney, elected annually by that body, and forty-five People's Deputies elected by constituencies delimited by parishes, as follows:

St Peter Port South	six Deputies
St Peter Port North	seven Deputies
St Sampson	six Deputies
Vale	seven Deputies
Castel	seven Deputies
West (St Saviour, St Pierre du Bois, Torteval, and Forest)	six Deputies
South-East (St Martin and St Andrew)	six Deputies

Under *The Reform (Guernsey) Law*, 1948, as amended, persons aged 17 years or over may have their names inscribed upon parochial electoral rolls, compiled every four years and updated annually. Any person on the roll who is aged 18 years and over, who has been ordinarily resident in Guernsey throughout the two years immediately preceding 31 October of the year of application, or for a period of five years in aggregate at any time preceding that date, and is not subject to any legal disability, is entitled to vote.

The Lieutenant-Governor has notice of and usually attends meetings of the States, where he is announced by H.M. Sheriff and sits immediately to the right of the Presiding Officer. He has no vote and is not known in modern times to have addressed the assembly, other than when leaving office. Meetings generally take place twelve times a year. The States follow rules of procedure approved under the Reform Law of 1948 at their meeting of 30 October 2003, which came into full effect on 1 May 2004. These cover matters such as routines for convening meetings, the roll call, the making of statements and asking of questions, order and rules of debate, *requêtes*,[9] amendments and *sursis*,[10] the

---

9. On which see p. 41, below.
10. Ie. acts deferring consideration of a matter brought before the States.

Register of Members' Interests, points of order, elections to Departments and Committees, etc.

The Conseillers

Under the 1948 Reform Law (which removed the Jurats and Rectors from the States) the States of Election elected twelve *Conseillers* as senior members of the States of Deliberation, serving terms of six years. In creating the office, the intention of the reformers had been (in the words of the second 'Carey Report' of 1991) 'to exercise a stabilising influence, to ensure continuity, to provide a nucleus of experienced persons, and to provide a "second" chamber within a unicameral system'.[11] Forty years later, many people felt that stability had been achieved, experienced politicians had been re-elected, and government had been 'conducted on a consensual rather than a confrontational basis'.[12] There was a movement for democratic change, and after receiving numerous reports in the period 1976–92, and reaching a variety of decisions, by *The Reform (Election of Conseillers and Minor Amendments) (Guernsey) Law*, 1993, the States introduced from 1 May 1994 universal adult suffrage in Guernsey and Alderney in elections of Conseillers to the States of Guernsey. After still further debate, *The Reform (Replacement of Conseillers) (Guernsey) Law*, 1998, finally abolished the office, with effect from 30 April 2000. Twelve more seats for People's Deputies were then introduced into the States. The Law of 1998 also extended the terms of office of all People's Deputies from three to four years.

---

11. The Report derived its popular title from the name of the President of the Constitution of the States Review Committee, de Vic G. Carey, Her Majesty's Procureur at the time. The first Carey Report, of 1986 (*Billet d'État* xviii, 29 October) addressed methods of election. The second, of 1991 (*Billet d'État* i, 30 January) unsuccessfully recommended abolition.

12. *Billet d'État* i, 1991 (30 January) 7. The *Report of the Committee of the Privy Council on Proposed Reforms in the Channel Islands* upon which this later report draws in dealing with the creation of the office (there designated 'Senator', a title that the States rejected in favour of 'Conseiller') added that '... many of the persons who would be well suited to the dignity of the office would be unwilling to conduct campaigns for public election. It was also represented to us that the electorate of the Island had not hitherto shown great interest in the business of the States, and that it would be a misfortune if the assembly lost the services of experienced men because the electorate was apathetic, or ignorant of the services which they had given to the Island.' (Privy Council, 1947 18).

Douzaine Representation

As stated in Chapter two, until the coming into force in 1844 of an Order in Council reforming the States, Parish Constables represented their Douzaines in the assembly. That Order substituted for the Constables fifteen Douzaine delegates, and so matters remained until *The Reform (Guernsey) Law*, 1948 reduced their number to ten, one representing each of Guernsey's parishes, appointed by their respective Douzaines, with Douzeniers and Constables being equally eligible for selection. The States voted on 17 May 2002, as part of the latest reform, to replace the position of Douzaine Representative with that of a 'Parish Representative', and extending the franchise for appointment to parishioners on the electoral roll. In reaching this outcome, the votes of the Representatives themselves were decisive. On 27 November 2002, this decision was reversed, and an effect of *The Reform (Guernsey) (Amendment) Law*, 2003, is that the States as constituted since 1 May 2004 no longer have delegates of the Douzaines as part of their number. There is no prohibition on People's Deputies combining membership of the States with Douzaine service – as there is in the case of the Jurats – and several Deputies do this.

The Committee system

For well over a century before 2004, for purposes of insular administration, the States were organised on a Committee basis. There were until 7 May that year a few more than forty Committees, constituted by legislation and/or States' resolutions, which set out their functions and mandates. Various divisions within Committees, for example the Island Archives Service, which was administered by the States' Heritage Committee, could similarly be mandated by resolution. States' meetings debated proposals embodied in policy letters brought by the Committees, occasionally with minority reports annexed, which were published in *Billets d'État*. The Committees, some of which had the titles of 'Authority', 'Board', or 'Council', administered areas of government including finance, the Civil Service, health, housing, planning, the police and other public services, tourism, transport, etc. They were accountable to the States. Committees met as often as necessary, some weekly, others quite rarely. With few exceptions, all standing States' Committees were served by presidents who had to be members of the States, and in

Committee deliberations exercised a casting but no original vote. Most Committees had six ordinary voting members, of whom only the majority had to be States' members, an arrangement allowing the import of a certain amount of additional expertise from lay members into discussions. The States elected presidents and members for three years, all of whom could stand for re-election.

The States' Advisory and Finance Committee

Before the recent reform of government, the leading States' Committee was the Advisory and Finance Committee, which had been established out of the States' Advisory Council and States' Finance Committee following a States' resolution of 23 January 1957.[13] Until its abolition at midnight on 6 May 2004, the Committee's constitution required the president and its six other members to be sitting States' members, with no lay membership. Its mandate was extensive, covering the formulation of objectives and implementation of policies co-ordinating the work of the States, the allocation of duties to Committees, establishing policies for the regulation of the financial services sector, the administration of constitutional arrangements, including international and Bailiwick relations, and the consideration of international agreements to which Guernsey was and still is invited to acquiesce. It provided Committees with services relating to finance, property, and information technology, and was responsible for the preparation of the States' annual budget and accounts. The Advisory and Finance Committee also administered resources for the Royal Court, and the offices of Crown appointees, including the Lieutenant-Governor, by virtue of the Jersey and Guernsey (Financial Provisions) Act 1947 and *The Lieutenant Governor (Salary and Official Expenses) Law*, 1948. It reviewed policy relating to the financial services sector of the economy, and surveyed population and migration statistics, considering any need for measures concerning them. It would propose policies to the States concerning all such matters, and also on criminal law reform measures, which were invariably recom-mended to the Committee by the Law Officers of the Crown. The Advisory and Finance Committee was particularly charged to receive and comment on all proposals and reports coming before the States,

---

13. See also *The States Advisory Council (Transfer of Functions) (Guernsey) Law*, 1957.

such views being published in *Billets d'État*. It could report to the States as it thought appropriate, and request any other Committee to report on any matter, even if the subject was not within the latter's mandate. With regard to international agreements, by reason of a States' resolution of 25 February 1987, the Advisory and Finance Committee was in some instances able to act independently, being permitted to make direct notification of acquiescence to certain agreements without first consulting the States. In other circumstances, however, consultation was required, for example, if proposals were regarded as controversial, related to human rights, or touched upon the concerns of particular States' Committees. The Advisory and Finance Committee was obliged to report to the States annually on all such agreements referred to it for consideration and actions the Committee had taken in relation to them. Nearly all of these important functions have now been transferred to the Policy Council and to the Treasury and Resources Department.

The reform of government

Under *The Machinery of Government (Transfer of Functions) (Guernsey) Ordinance*, 2003,[14] made in pursuance of States' Resolutions of 16 May 2003 and 31 October 2003, with effect from midnight on 6 May 2004, the functions, rights, and liabilities of States' Committees and their presidents were transferred to new Departments and Ministers (and, to an extent, new Committees, to which we turn in due course). The new structure of government was the outcome of a process of investigation, consultation, and intense debate that had commenced nearly five years before, when by resolution of 10 December 1998, the States appointed an independent panel to review the machinery of government in Guernsey, under the chairmanship of Advocate Peter Harwood. This recommended the introduction of an executive form of government, with a Chief Minister, who would select the Ministers responsible for proposed new Departments. All Ministers would sit on a Council, and have extensive powers. The Harwood Panel also proposed new electoral districts, and a reduction in the number of States' members. The States' Advisory and Finance Committee and Procedures and Constitution Committee reviewed the findings and recommendations of the Panel and made a

---

14. Brought into effect by *The Machinery of Government (Transfer of Functions) (Guernsey) Ordinance, 2003 (Commencement) Ordinance*, 2004.

variety of proposals for decision by the States. The outcome of several States' meetings, the most significant of which took place in May, October, and November 2002, and May and October 2003, was a rejection of the proposed executive style of government, and the maintenance of the States' collegiate and consensual character, but the acceptance – with some modifications – of several of the other proposals.

Accordingly, new electoral districts have been created, the removal of the Douzaine Representatives has reduced the number of States' Members by ten, the manner of the Chief Minister's and Ministers' election and appointment have been implemented, and the title and non-voting powers of the Presiding Officer established. Since 7 May 2004 the States have been organised into ten Departments, each served by a Minister appointed by States' vote. Each Minister is also *ex officio* a member of the Policy Council, which is chaired by the Chief Minister, also elected by States' vote, and who has the right to make the first proposals in elections of Ministers, and to determine the order in which elections of Ministers takes place. The Chief Minister and all Ministers and members of Departments hold office for terms of four years, and all are eligible for re-election. The constitutions and mandates of the Policy Council, the Departments, and the Committees of the States, as approved by Resolution of the States of 31 October 2003, which have been in effect from 7 May 2004, and as provided for by *The Machinery of Government (Transfer of Functions) (Guernsey) Ordinance*, 2003, and other enabling legislation and resolutions, are summarised and digested in the following few pages.[15]

The Policy Council

Each Minister has a seat on the Policy Council, which is presided over by the Chief Minister, who may not head a Department. Neither may Ministers preside over more than one Department. The Chief Minister is responsible for the preparation and presentation of corporate policies to the States, and for leading the development of cross-departmental policies, through the creation of sub-groups of the Policy Council, which may include relevant Ministers, and also co-opted representatives of

---

15. In several respects, these reproduce almost *verbatim* Appendices 2,3,4, and 5 of *Billet d'État* xxiv 2003 (29 October) which were subjects of the resolution of 31 October 2003.

non-government organisations and private businesses. The Chief Minister is also responsible for overseeing policy and resource plans that are endorsed by the Policy Council before presentation to the States for approval, and also for negotiating and speaking politically for Guernsey, with the Policy Council's authority and as mandated by the States. The Deputy Chief Minister is elected by the States from amongst the Ministers, and, whilst retaining his or her own departmental responsibilities, is also Deputy Chief Minister of the Policy Council and deputises in the Chief Minister's absence.

The Policy Council operates according to consensus, or by majority voting, as necessary. The Chief Minister (or whoever else is presiding) has an original but no casting vote, and any tied vote is declared lost. The Council has a mandate to advise the States on matters relating to Guernsey's constitutional position including its relationships with the United Kingdom, the European Union, and the other Crown Dependencies, international relations, and matters relating to the parishes and the other islands of the Bailiwick. It is to see to the formulation and implementation of economic, fiscal, human resource, environmental, social strategic, and corporate policies, to meet objectives agreed by the States, and generally to coordinate the work of the States. Its responsibilities for constitutional affairs include representing Guernsey (but not Alderney or Sark) and negotiating on international matters, considering international agreements in which the insular authorities have an interest or to which they are invited to acquiesce, and making appropriate recommendations thereon, in the same manner as was done by the Advisory and Finance Committee. The Council oversees the relationship between the States of Guernsey and of Alderney, and provides, on behalf of the former, hospitality to appropriate visiting persons and organizations, and formulates policy for the provision of aid overseas. In terms of strategic and corporate policy the Policy Council is responsible for developing, together with the relevant Departments, appropriate responses to issues that confront Guernsey, including any population and migration measures considered necessary, and the policy framework for the regulation of the financial services sector. Subsuming some of the functions of the former Civil Service Board, the Policy Council operates a corporate human resource policy, addressing terms and conditions of employment, compliance with legislation and good practice, and it is responsible for the provision of employment services and advice to Departments and Committees as appropriate, also fulfilling the States' role as employer of established staff. It appoints the chief officers of Departments and Committees and other senior civil servants, and sanctions the recommendations of the Public Sector Remuneration Committee in respect of the posts of the Lieutenant-Governor, Bailiff, Deputy Bailiff, Law Officers of the Crown, and Magistrates, also determining the remuneration and conditions of service applicable to Her Majesty's Greffier, Sheriff, and Sergeant, after consultation with Her Majesty's Procureur. The Policy Council is also mandated with the provision of research programmes and the maintenance of certain statistics, including responsibility for population data. It coordinates States' activities, and allocates responsibilities and functions to Departments and Committees. The coordination of non-operational matters in the event of an emergency, to preserve life and the well being of the community, including under *The Emergency Powers (Bailiwick of Guernsey) (Law)*, 1965, and the preservation of law and order generally are also the Council's responsibility. It may require a Department or Committee to examine and report to the States concerning any matter which falls within or without the mandate of such a Department or Committee. The Policy Council, again in place of the former Advisory and Finance Committee, also receives and comments as appropriate on all proposals and reports which are to be placed before the States by Departments and Committees, publishing these as appropriate in *Billets d'État*. The preparation of the agenda for meetings of the States of Deliberation and Election are within the Council's mandate (though these are convened by the Presiding Officer), as are the prioritisation of the States' legislative programme, and responsibility for the Island Archives Service.

The new Departments

The Departments of the States are each constituted by a Minister and four members, all of whom must be sitting Members of the States, and elected by the States, and up to two non-voting members, appointed by the Department, who cannot be sitting members of the States. As with the Policy Council, the person presiding at meetings has an original but no casting vote (tied votes are declared lost). The Departments' main activities may be summarized as follows:

(a)   The Treasury and Resources Department is mandated to advise the States on matters relating to the allocation and administration of all States' resources, the regulation and control of the States' financial affairs, and the raising of States' income, and control of financial resources. It also advises on systems for the assessment and collection of income tax, and tax on rateable value, and is responsible for examining and submitting annually to the States the budget estimates of income and expenditure on capital and revenue account, submitting recommendations as to how such expenditure should be financed and, after audit, submitting the annual accounts to the States. The Department receives and comments as appropriate on the resource implications associated with all proposals and reports that are to be placed before the States by Departments and Committees. Its responsibilities also include financial and related functions, including the States' payroll and the provision of advice and services to Departments and Committees, the management of financial assets including cash and other investments, and associated financial activities, authorising Departments and Committees to borrow, and to make loans or grants to charities and similar organisations. The Department also maintains the register of property ownership for the purpose of assessing and collecting taxes based on rateable value, and provides property and procurement services and advice to Departments and Committees, and internal audit, risk management and insurance of States' activities and resources. The Department is also charged with the development of policies concerning the States' use of information and communication technology, the administration of the staff number limitation policy, the shareholders' functions and duties in respect of the States' trading companies and other States-owned entities, and the provision of resources for the offices of Crown appointees and for the functions of the Royal Court. Altogether, the Treasury and Resources Department exercises many of the powers and duties which were those of the former Advisory and Finance Committee, Board of Administration, Cadastre Committee, Civil Service Board, and Income Tax Authority;

(b)   The Commerce and Employment Department is responsible for advising the States on economic development matters, and promoting all sectors of the economy, both domestically and internationally, including the financial services sector, and tourism. It deals with the States' Dairy, farming, and sea fisheries, regulates certain utilities, and promotes good employment practices and policies, industrial relations, health and safety at work, and consumer protection. The Department also sets trading standards;

(c)   The Culture and Leisure Department is mandated to advise the States on the promotion of, and is responsible for, arts and crafts, and all sport and recreation facilities, the States' museums and galleries, and the historical and archaeological sites in its care. It liaises with, and has oversight of, the Guernsey Sports Commission, promotes and administers public lotteries, including the use of proceeds, and also plans and implements arrangements to mark Guernsey's annual celebration of Liberation Day;[16]

(d)   The Education Department advises the States on matters relating to, and is responsible for, education (including vocational and industrial training) in Guernsey, Alderney and Herm, youth organizations, grant-aided colleges, and the libraries. It provides assistance for students taking courses of education and training, and is responsible for a variety of educational and support services;

(e)   The Environment Department advises the States on environmental policy relating to matters including transport, energy, waste, conservation, and the enhancement and development of the environment, and on environmental monitoring. It is responsible for protection, conservation, enhancement, and land use strategies, including those relating to the management of transport, energy, and natural resources, and waste disposal. Its transport policy remit includes traffic management, road safety, the coordination of road closures, and the regulation of public transport. It processes development applications, whether concerning planning, building control, protected buildings, or

---

16. Liberation Day, celebrated on 9 May, is effectively Guernsey's national holiday. It marks the surrender, on 9 May 1945, of the forces that occupied Guernsey during the Second World War.

scheduled sites. It is also the authority for vehicle registration, and vehicle and driver licensing, and it manages States' interests in the islands of Herm and Jethou (see pp. 101–02);

(f) The Health and Social Services Department advises the States on the mental, physical, and social well being of the people of Guernsey and Alderney. It is responsible for promoting, protecting, and improving personal, environmental, and public, health and preventing or diagnosing and treating illness, disease and disability, and caring for the sick, old, infirm, and those with disabilities. It provides social services including ensuring the welfare and protection of children;

(g) The Home Department advises the States on criminal justice policy, as developed and reviewed in consultation with the Courts, Law Officers, and other interested parties, and also advises on broadcasting, and gambling. It is responsible for the Island Police Force, the Customs and Immigration Service, and financial intelligence. It administers immigration and nationality controls, the issue of passports, the import and export of goods and the collection of duties thereon. It maintains the Prison Service, the Attendance Centre for young offenders, and the States' Probation Service, and provides certain services to the Courts and others, also liaising with the Parole Review Committee and providing administrative services to it.[17] The Home Department is also responsible for the Fire Brigade and fire fighting, fire safety, rescue, and salvage, and the development, testing, and maintenance of emergency response plans, including Civil Defence. It also administers the electoral roll and liaises with the Data Protection Office;

(h) The Housing Department advises the States on matters relating to housing needs, and is responsible for the coordination and direction of programmes, and the provision and management of housing administered by the States, including administration of the States' Houses Fund. It facilitates and supports the development of affordable housing, including the regulation

---

17. Created under *The Parole Review Committee (Guernsey) Law*, 1989, and subject to *The Parole Review Committee Ordinance*, 1991, as amended (most recently by *The Parole Review Committee (Amendment) Ordinance*, 2004), with such a constitution as from time to time may be determined by States' resolution.

and funding of housing associations and other bodies, and administers the States' Housing Development and Loans Fund to provide financial assistance for house purchase and repair. The Department is also charged with establishing initiatives to improve the affordability and quality of the private rental sector, including the administration of *The Rent Control (Guernsey) Law*, 1976. It operates controls on housing occupation through the relevant laws, and manages two retirement homes;

(i) The Public Services Department advises the States on the management of publicly-owned infrastructure and the provision of public services, including Guernsey and Alderney airports, St Peter Port and St Sampson's harbours, the roads, waste and drainage networks, and the public water supply, Alderney's breakwater, and maritime affairs generally. The Department provides facilities and services in respect of those airports and harbours, supplies coast guard services, maintains the Guernsey Register of British ships, and surveys and licenses vessels, monitoring compliance within Bailiwick waters with international and local laws. It is responsible for maritime safety, the investigation of marine accidents, provision of navigational aids, and safety information. It liaises with the Guernsey branch of the Royal National Lifeboat Institution, and oversees pilotage services. It maintains lanes and roads, keeping these clean, and manages, collects, and disposes of water thereon and thereunder. It arranges the management, collection, treatment, and disposal of wastes, and manages environmental emergencies, and the receivership of wrecks. It provides engineering and architectural services, and also maintains the Alderney breakwater, and maintains and manages a cemetery and crematorium, public conveniences, the States' markets, and buildings on Herm, also providing a direct labour organisation, namely the States Works Department;

(j) As its name suggests, the Social Security Department advises the States on matters relating to the provision of social security, through social, health, and long-term care insurances and other schemes of social protection, for the well being of Guernsey and Alderney residents, and for migrant workers and their families. It provides through the Parochial Outdoor Assistance Boards temporary financial support to persons whose resources are insufficient to meet basic living standards, and is responsible for the collection of, and accountable for, social security contributions, and the payment of social security benefits and grants. It controls and manages the Guernsey Insurance Fund, the Guernsey Health Service Fund, and the Long-term Care Insurance Fund.

The new Committees

A States' Resolution of 31 October 2003, made under *The States Committees (Constitution and Amendment) (Guernsey) Law*, 1991, created five standing Committees, in addition to the new Departments.[18] Each of the new Committees has a chairman and members, voting in the same manner as those of the Departments, similarly serving terms of four years, and also constituted with effect from 7 May 2004. They are:

(a) The House Committee, which has a chairman, and four members, all five of whom are required to be sitting members of the States. The Committee's mandate requires it to review and bring forward proposals for the States to consider in connection with the constitutions of the States of Deliberation and the States of Election, and the Rules of Procedure of the former, the constitution and operation of States' Departments and Committees, the system of election of Ministers and Members of Departments and Committees, and matters relating to the functioning of the States in both forms, and also elections to the office of People's Deputy, and matters relating to the propriety and conduct of States Members once elected. It advises on training and support for Members, and general procedures for the management of public business in the States. The Presiding Officer and Her Majesty's Greffier are entitled to attend meetings of the House Committee to advise on matters relating to rules of procedure and the functioning of the States, as provided for by Section 14 (5) of the States' Resolution of 31 October 2003;

---

18. The Resolution also continued the Inheritance Law Review Committee as a Special States' Committee, and confirmed States' participation in The Ladies' College Board of Governors, the Parochial Outdoor Assistance Boards, the Priaulx Library Council, and the Elizabeth College Board of Directors.

(b) The Legislation Select Committee, which is constituted by a chairman, and four members, all five of whom are required to be sitting members of the States, with the addition of up to two non-voting members appointed by the Committee who must not be sitting members of the States. The Committee's mandate obliges it to review and revise every *Projet de Loi* presented to it by either Law Officer of the Crown (often represented by a Crown Advocate)[19] for the purpose of ensuring accordance with, and that it will effectually carry into effect, any resolution of the States, and to transmit it to the States for consideration and decision. It similarly treats draft Ordinances brought before it by either Law Officer (again often represented by a Crown Advocate) at the instance of the States, or of some Authority, Board, Committee or Council of the States, and transmits the same to the States for consideration and decision, save in the case of any draft where the Committee regards immediate or early enactment to be in the public interest. In such circumstances, the Committee has the significant power to order that the same shall be operative either immediately or at such a date as the Committee shall prescribe, provided that every Ordinance coming into effect in such a way is laid before the States as soon as may be after its making. This power is used, for example, to ensure that international sanctions legislation is enacted expeditiously or, more prosaically, to correct drafting errors in existing Ordinances. If, when the Ordinance is laid before the States, the States resolve that it should be annulled, then it ceases to have effect. The Legislation Select Committee is also mandated to study, together with the Standing Committee of the Guernsey Deanery Synod, schemes for the application of General Synod measures prepared by the Bishop of Winchester, under the Channel Islands (Church Legislation) Measure 1931, as amended, and to report on them to the States. It may also suggest to the Policy Council matters that might require changes to legislation;

---

19. As provided for by Rule 14 (4) of the Resolution of 31 October 2003.

(c) The Public Sector Remuneration Committee which comprises a chairman, and four members, all five of whom are required to be sitting members of the States, with the addition of up to two non-voting members appointed by the Committee, who must not be sitting members of the States. They together are responsible for collective bargaining, on behalf of the States as employer, in respect of the pay and conditions of service of States' employees, and the review of the remuneration of the Lieutenant-Governor, Bailiff, Deputy Bailiff, Law Officers of the Crown, and Magistrates. The Committee makes recommendations concerning the pensions and other benefits due under the Public Servants' Pension Scheme, and the Teachers' Superannuation Scheme;

(d) The Scrutiny Committee, which has a chairman, and eight members, who all are required to be sitting members of the States. Its mandate requires the Committee, through a process of political scrutiny, to subject Departments and Committees to regular reviews, with a particular emphasis on determining the effectiveness of their policies and the services they provide, and identifying areas that might be addressed inadequately or inappropriately. The Scrutiny Committee is also to identify new areas of policy or service that may require implementation, and determine how well a new policy, service, or project has been implemented. It promotes changes in policies and services where persuaded that these require amendment, and reviews issues and matters of public importance, in particular liaising with the Public Accounts Committee to ensure appropriate coordination of the scrutiny process; and

(e) The Public Accounts Committee, which comprises a chairman who must be a sitting States' member and eight members, four of who are sitting members of the States, and four who are not. Taking on the responsibilities of the former States' Audit Commission,[20] it ensures that proper scrutiny is given to the

---

20. A States' Audit Commission was established under *The States Audit Commission (Guernsey) Law,* 1997. It was abolished with effect from 6 May 2004 under *The States Audit Commission (Guernsey) (Repeal) Law,* 2004. The Commission's function had been to oversee the internal auditing of States' interests, to receive external audits on the same, monitor standards, policies, and procedures, assist Committees in the management of finances and to report to the Advisory and Finance Committee in relation to such matters. Whilst the Commission was an

States' assets, expenditure and revenues, so that States' bodies operate to high standards in the management of financial affairs, and examines whether public funds have been applied for the intended purposes and that waste and extravagance are eliminated. The Committee will recommend to the States the appointment of the States' external auditors, and liaise with the Scrutiny Committee to ensure appropriate coordination of the scrutiny process.

The Chief Executive of the States of Guernsey and the States as employer

In 1563, the Crown granted the Royal Court certain harbour revenues, known as the *Petit Coutume*.[21] From 1611 the administration both of these monies (the right to the receipt of which from the 1780s was farmed) and of the harbour was annually delegated to one or another of the Jurats, who assumed the title of *Superviseur de la Chaussée* for that year. From the 1850s, the annual character of the office disappeared, and in 1920 the Royal Court yielded the right of appointment to the States. In 1922 the latter body resolved that the office should no longer be held by one of its members, but be a Civil Service post. By this time, the title had been anglicised to *States' Supervisor*, and the appointee charged with far wider responsibilities than just managing the harbour and its income.[22] Articles three and four of *The Machinery of Government (Transfer of Functions) (Guernsey) Ordinance*, 2003, incorporated this ancient office into the newly created office of 'Chief Executive of the States of Guernsey'.

In 1824, an Assistant Supervisor was first appointed. A States' Office was established in 1831.[23] From such beginnings the Civil Service developed. It presently employs some 1,800 people. A further 3,000 or so

---

agency of the States, without a separate legal personality, it was not a Committee of the States, and not subject to Committee rules, nor did it enjoy Committee privileges. It had independent powers to require public exposure of matters of exceptional importance, and reported annually in respect of its functions.

21. Ogier, 1996 65. The *Petit Coutume* was abolished in 1851 and the Royal Court compensated with an annual payment from the States (Hocart, 1988 49).
22. Hocart, 1988 8, 10, 80, 97.
23. Hocart, 1988 53.

work for States' Departments, in manual work, the nursing and teaching professions, and in the Police and Customs services.[24] A States' Civil Service Board, first established in 1963, was responsible for many aspects of the States' role as an employer, and its responsibilities have now been transferred to the Policy Council and the Public Sector Remuneration Committee.

The Chief Executive of the States of Guernsey is the senior States' officer and head of the civil service. In 1970, the States' Supervisor became chief executive of the States' Advisory and Finance Committee, and, under the new title, he retains that role in relation to the Policy Council, which he advises on policy, including with regard to proposals from States' Departments and Committees. In administrative affairs, he liaises with the chief officers of the various States' Departments and Committees, and may attend their meetings as necessary. The Chief Executive of the States of Guernsey will also, save in respect of the Policy Council, carry out preliminary investigations in cases where Departments and Committees appear to be failing in their responsibilities, and where administrative acts are complained of, under *The Administrative Decisions (Review) (Guernsey) Law*, 1986, as amended.

The States and the Law

From time immemorial, until the reforms of 1948, the Royal Court had legislative functions, with power to make Ordinances (*Ordonnances*) which, although they could not impose tax nor directly alter superior legislation, operated to regulate what an Order in Council of 1568 referred to as 'the good government, surety and quietness' of island life.[25] Though it was a commonplace that Ordinances could not alter the customary law, they did sometimes purport to declare it, for example with regard to usufruct,[26] the distinction between immovable and moveable property,[27] or the possibility of hypothecating certain move-

---

24. Edwards, 1998 iii 6. These figures cannot have changed much since the time of the Edwards Report, because the States impose a staff numbers limitation policy, administered by the Treasury and Resources Department.
25. Commission 1846, 1848 xii.
26. Ordinance of 16 January 1854.
27. Ordinance of 19 January 1852, and see also an Ordinance of 1 October 1888, on the status of tomatoes and early potatoes.

ables.[28] For a century before 1948,[29] Ordinances might be provisional and technically effective for just a year (*Ordonnances provisoire*), though in practice, many were renewed wholesale at sittings of Chief Pleas after Christmas, or they might be permanent, by virtue of an enabling law, or because they had been made permanent by the Royal Court following the approval of the States. The States themselves had no power to make such regulations. Some States' Committees submitted Ordinances for promulgation by the Court. The Court, following requests embodied in States' resolutions, created others. Although the contrary had been the case historically, few Ordinances originated with the Court itself. Should proposed Ordinances provoke controversy, expressed at Chief Pleas or elsewhere, the Court would refer them to the States.

Imposing a tax or amending the written law beyond what was susceptible to regulation by Ordinance required Privy Council consent. This was largely the responsibility of the States. A States' resolution was drawn up by the Law Officers and brought before the Royal Court, with the request that a draft law (*Projet de Loi*) be prepared. The Law Officers drafted this too. The Court would submit the *Projet* to the States for review, and, if necessary, modification. (Objections to the Court of the sort allowed against proposed Ordinances were not permissible, since it considered itself bound by States' resolution). The *Projet* was then transmitted to the Privy Council for sanction, and the subsequent Order in Council, upon registration by the Royal Court, became law, immediately or at a date provided for.[30]

The previous two paragraphs supply the background to modern practice. *The Reform (Guernsey) Law, 1948,* transferred very nearly all of the Royal Court's legislative powers to the States.[31] This made the States responsible not only for the creation of *Projets de Loi*, but also of all Ordinances. Legislation is generally only drafted after the acceptance of an 'in principle' decision approving the particular proposal to legislate

---

28. Ordinance of 25 April 1636.
29. *Billet d'État* v 1848 (18 August) and resolution thereon.
30. Sherwill, 1946 238–39.
31. The Royal Court may still make orders and rules of procedure for the courts. The 1948 Law had also reserved to the Royal Court the power to make defence regulations, but these were transferred to the States' Emergency Council by Article 27 of *The Reform (Guernsey) (Amendment) Law, 2003,* and the functions of the Emergency Council were transferred to the Policy Council under *The Machinery of Government (Transfer of Functions) (Guernsey) Ordinance, 2003.*

and directing the preparation of legislation, following the submission of a report by a States' Department or Committee addressed to the Policy Council and published in a *Billet d'État*. In cases of urgency, the Policy Council may be asked to agree to a draft *Projet* being tabled at the same time as the report. Exceptionally a petition (*requête*) signed by at least seven States' members and brought before a States' meeting may also lead to the creation of new legislation, most commonly by asking a States' Department to investigate a matter, report on it, and to produce a draft law. Save in instances where the proposal comes from the Policy Council and/or the Treasury and Resources Department, the report usually is accompanied by an opinion from one or both of those bodies as to whether the States should accept the proposals, sometimes also suggesting qualifications or modifications. If it forms the opinion that a report or *requête* in a *Billet* does not comply with the corporate policy of the States, the Policy Council may defer its inclusion until the next meeting of the States. Once any report or *requête* does come before the States, it is debated, and any amendments are considered. Assuming the proposals are not rejected altogether, or consideration deferred by *sursis*, then the States direct the preparation of such legislation as may be necessary to give effect to their decision.

In the case of a law or amendment requiring the sanction of Her Majesty in Council, the legal draftsmen of the Chambers of the Law Officers of the Crown then produce a *Projet de Loi*, which is submitted to the Legislation Select Committee. The *Projet* is then brought before a States' meeting and members are asked if they are of opinion to approve it and to authorise the Bailiff to petition Her Majesty in Council to sanction the same. Approval is usually, though not invariably, given without debate. The Bailiff's Office then transmits the *Projet* to the Privy Council, *via* the Lieutenant-Governor. A report on it by one of the Law Officers of the Crown to the Lieutenant-Governor accompanies the *Projet*. No Lieutenant-Governor of modern times is known to have commented officially on such a report. The Department for Constitutional Affairs examines the *Projet*, and sometimes – where particular interests, for example fisheries, are engaged – will invite the views of other United Kingdom Government departments. From the Department for Constitutional Affairs, it is transmitted to the Committee of the Privy Council for the Affairs of Guernsey and Jersey, which recommends its approval and ratification. Royal Sanction is then given, and an Order in

Council embodying the *Projet* is made. The Order is transmitted to the Royal Court, with a direction that it be entered upon the Register of the island of Guernsey. It is presented to the Court by one of the Law Officers and registration follows. It may come into force immediately, at a date appointed in the Order, or later, often being brought in by Ordinance of the States, or in parts, by a succession of Ordinances of the States. *The Taxes and Duties (Provisional Effect) (Guernsey) Law*, 1992, allows the States to bring in by resolution taxes, duties, and related legislation, before sanction by Her Majesty in Council and registration by the Royal Court. Further power today is regularly delegated to the States under other Orders in Council, enabling the making of amendments and subsidiary legislation by Ordinance, so as to change the law without further recourse to the Privy Council.[32]

The procedure when the States make Ordinances is less complicated. Here, matters follow a course similar to that bringing about Orders in Council, as far as the point where a States' meeting approves the draft legislation (amendment, deferral, or rejection are also possibilities). Should the draft Ordinance be approved, the States then simply direct that the same should have effect as an Ordinance of the States, immediately or at a specified date. Under the 1948 Reform Law, no Ordinances of the States have the annual character of some of the old *Ordonnances* of the Royal Court, but are permanent.

Privilege

In 2000, the opinion was expressed that members enjoyed qualified privilege in respect of statements made in the States of Deliberation, conferring limited protection in respect of words honestly published without malice. Whether they enjoyed absolute privilege, conferring a complete defence to proceedings for defamation, was unclear, and untested judicially.[33] A States' Meeting of 29 October 2003 therefore directed that legislation be enacted establishing the principle of absolute

---

32. Including as respects non-human rights compliant sections of Orders in Council, once *The Human Rights (Implementation and Amendment) (Bailiwick of Guernsey) Law*, 2004, approved at a States' meeting of 26 May 2004, has been brought into force.

33. Rowland, 2000 125–26. With regard to qualified privilege the opinion there expressed partly draws on a judgment of the Court of Alderney in *Wells v Hammond*,

privilege with regard to their proceedings, providing that 'no civil or criminal proceedings may be instituted against any Member of the States for words spoken before or written in a report to, the States or a Department or Committee of the States, or by reason of any matter or thing brought by him [*or her*] therein by *requête*, proposition or otherwise'. Breaches or abuses of the privilege will be susceptible to reprimand, suspension, or expulsion of offending members.[34]

The wider review of States' activities

The decisions and acts of the States and their Departments, Committees, and servants are subject to supervision and review not only by the Public Accounts Committee and the Scrutiny Committee, as described above, but also by a number of other bodies, including:

(a) Review Boards
    The Administrative Decisions (Review) (Guernsey) Law, 1986 set up procedures enabling persons aggrieved by decisions and acts that are now made and done by States' Departments and Committees to apply to the Chief Executive of the States of Guernsey (or H.M. Greffier in respect of complaints against the Policy Council) for consideration by a Review Board. The Law was enacted in the absence at the time of a judicial review system, such as existed in the United Kingdom, to provide a solution tailored to Guernsey's consensus-based system of government. Administrative Decision Review Boards are constituted from a panel consisting of States' Members of more than three years' standing and the Deans of all the Douzaines. Boards have no statutory power to enforce their findings, but rather, upon finding the subject matter of a complaint to be illegal, unjust, mistaken, unreasonable, or contrary to natural justice, will seek to persuade Departments and Committees to amend affairs, failing which the matter is referred to a States' meeting. Following the introduction of judicial review procedures into Guernsey law, treated below, it was anticipated that Review Boards would be convened less

---

recited in full in the *Guernsey Evening Press and Star* of 2 May 1970. With regard to absolute privilege, see the judgment of the Judicial Committee of the Privy Council in the case of *Chenard v Arissol* [1949] AC 127, cited in Rowland, 2000 126.
34. *Billet d'État* xxi 2003 (26 September).

frequently than has been the case in the past, and in fact upon the creation of an independent Tribunals Service, as also described below, the present Review Board system will be abolished altogether;

(b) Tribunals
In 1949, a tribunal appointed by the States to investigate an allegation of corruption in the Civil Service abandoned its task in view of its inability to summon witnesses, examine them on oath, compel the production of documents, or offer privileges and immunities similar to those enjoyed by witnesses before the Royal Court. As a remedy to such problems, the *Tribunals of Inquiry (Evidence) (Guernsey) Law*, 1949 was made, on the model of the United Kingdom's Tribunals of Enquiry (Evidence) Act 1921. The occasional enquiries that have taken place under the Law (which was subject to minor technical amendment in 1957) have often had planning and development issues as their subjects. Besides the general power created under the Law of 1949, other enactments provide for tribunals in respect of particular Departments' activities.

Mindful of human rights considerations and the piecemeal nature of the existing systems, the States in 2002 resolved to create an independent Tribunals Service, to take on all existing (extra-judicial) review powers, and to deal with appeals from certain non-governmental bodies such as the Guernsey Financial Services Commission[35] and the Douzaines. It is proposed that the chairman and deputy chairman of the Tribunals Service are to be legally-qualified, and on matters of law a right of appeal to

---

35. In the mid nineteen-eighties, the States noted the growth of the contribution of the financial services sector to Guernsey's economy. There was an awareness of the sector's international character, the need to maintain confidence internationally, within a properly supervised structure, and of its complexity and rapid reaction to events. This awareness led to the implementation of *The Financial Services Commission (Bailiwick of Guernsey) Law*, 1987, creating the Guernsey Financial Services Commission. The Commission is not a committee nor servant or agent of the States, but a body corporate with perpetual succession and a common seal, which may sue and be sued. The Commission's purpose is to regulate financial business in the Bailiwick, with functions including advising the Policy Council with regard to instruments and legislation. The Commission also has powers under *The Financial Services Commission (Bailiwick of Guernsey) Law*, 1987, as amended, to regulate

the Royal Court from its decisions should exist. The composition of panels will vary as to numbers of members, and some members should have expertise in matters under review; and

(c) the Courts
Alongside this pending statutory alteration, the Courts have recently developed the law of Guernsey in a manner that allows the judicial review of administrative decisions. This follows a decision of 14 December 1998 of the Guernsey Court of Appeal to grant leave to appeal in the matter of *Bassington Limited and others v H.M. Procureur*. Subsequently, the Royal Court and the Guernsey Court of Appeal have entertained judicial review cases.[36]

Human Rights

The introduction of domestic provisions relating to human rights is also imminent, and will constitute a further influence on States' business and the interpretation of legislation.

The European Court of Human Rights, which is a Council of Europe institution, was established in 1953. It sits at Strasbourg, and its function is to secure the enforcement of the obligations of states contracted to the European Convention for the Protection of Human Rights and Fundamental Freedoms. The Convention was opened for signature in Rome on 4 November 1950, and ratified by the United Kingdom on 8

---

banking, insurance and investment business, and, under *The Regulation of Fiduciaries, Administration Businesses and Company Directors, etc. (Bailiwick of Guernsey) Law*, 2000, regulates businesses in those areas.
36.   For example in the matter of *Barrett and Barrett v the Island Development Committee and Osprey Investments Limited*. The judgments of the Royal Court (of 1 July 2003) and of the Court of Appeal (of 18 December 2003) in this matter may conveniently be accessed in *Billet d'État* iii 2004 (10 March). In his judgment of 9 December 2003 in the case *Old Government House Hotel Limited v The President of the Island Development Committee (Mighty Mouse Limited intervening)* Lieutenant-Bailiff Day stated '. . . I can positively express the view, which I know is shared by my judicial colleagues, that the remedy [of judicial review] is unquestionably available in this jurisdiction'. A recent judgment of the Royal Court (Patrick J. Talbot, QC, Lieutenant-Bailiff, sitting alone), of 29 June 2004 in the matter of *Jersey Fishermen's Association Limited, If Limited, Interfish Wirons Limited, Scerene Fishing Company Limited and Lovell v The States of Guernsey* set aside an Ordinance of the States as unlawful and of no effect. An appeal has been lodged.

March 1951. It came into force in September 1953, and on 23 October 1953 was extended to Guernsey, by means of a notification made to the Secretary General of the Council of Europe, in accordance with practice at the time. The Royal Court registered the Convention on 9 February 1971.

In 1966, the United Kingdom recognised the entitlement of its citizens to petition against alleged breaches of Convention rights by contracting states, and accepted that with regard to complaints reaching the Court of Human Rights for a final ruling, that judgment would be binding. These provisions extend to individuals and groups in Guernsey, and the Court of Human Rights may hear cases of alleged breaches of the Convention by the States of Guernsey, once domestic remedies have been exhausted. These domestic remedies are soon to be extended, upon the introduction of the Convention into island law by *The Human Rights (Bailiwick of Guernsey) Law*, 2000, and *The Human Rights (Implementation and Amendment) (Bailiwick of Guernsey) Law*, 2004, both of which are due to be brought into force by Ordinance. The effect of these will be to enable some Bailiwick courts to take Convention provisions into account in legal proceedings, and to offer remedies.[37] The laws also require the acts of public authorities, including courts and tribunals, and of persons carrying out functions of a public nature, to be compatible with Convention rights, unless primary legislation precludes this – the States of Guernsey and the other Bailiwick legislatures (the States of Alderney and Sark's Chief Pleas) are exempt in that regard, in order to preserve their necessary parliamentary sovereignty – and allows the Royal Court and Court of Appeal to make declarations of legislative incompatibility, as a *Billet d'État* considered at a States' meeting of 5 April 2000 spelled out

> ... The Courts will be required to interpret legislation so as to uphold the Convention rights unless the legislation itself is so clearly incompatible with the Convention that it is impossible to do so.
>
> This 'rule of construction' is to apply to past as well as to future legislation. To the extent that it affects the meaning of a legislative provision, the courts will not be bound by previous interpretations.

---

37. The *Projet de Loi* of *The Human Rights (Implementation and Amendment) (Bailiwick of Guernsey) Law*, 2004 was approved at a States' meeting of 26 May 2004, and awaits Royal sanction.

They will be able to build a new body of case law, taking into account the Convention rights. In doing so, they will give enactments a broad and general construction, adopting European interpretations, rather than a strict, 'black letter' legalistic approach which has been the traditional foundation of English and Guernsey law. ...[38]

These represent new influences upon the activities of States' Departments and Committees, and upon the creation and content of legislation.

Referenda

On 1 August 2002, the States directed the preparation of legislation allowing the holding of referenda in Guernsey. The Advisory and Finance Committee's policy letter that recommended such a course asserted that because geographical boundaries 'are less important than they once were', a time might come when 'major decisions may have to be made concerning the island's constitutional future'. The States' meeting resolved that other matters of importance, not extending to the international, might also be the subject of referenda, and voted to provide for this. It also decided that the power of proposing a referendum should not be limited to the Advisory and Finance Committee (and so it is not now limited to the Policy Council) and that when resolving to call a referendum, the States should at such time decide whether the outcome should be binding upon them.

Reviewing reform

These are early days for the new Departments and Committees, and the *Billet d'État* setting out their proposed mandates recognised that, as the new machinery of government evolves, some review and amendment by the States may be necessary. With this in mind, the Policy Council is to review the new system once this has been running for a year. Alongside these alterations, Guernsey's domestic law is continuing to evolve, and relations with the United Kingdom, Europe, and the wider world are also changing, as described, amongst other things, in following chapters.

---

38. *Billet d'État* ix, 2000 (5 April) 497. Cf. *Billet d'État* ii, 2004 (25 Feb.) 112–113 concerning the enabling of the States to amend a non-compliant provision by Ordinance.

5. The Courts

The Royal Court

The Royal Court is presided over by the Bailiff of Guernsey, and when it sits as a Full Court (historically described as the *Cour en Corps*) is constituted by the Bailiff, or a presiding judge performing his functions,[1] and at least seven Jurats, and as an Ordinary Court is comprised of the Bailiff and at least two Jurats.

The Full Court

The Full Court sits in sessions of Chief Pleas (*Chefs Plaids*) and also with criminal, licensing, review, and appeal functions. It also swears in officers, and supervises disciplinary matters referred to it by the *Chambre de Discipline* (see pp. 76–77).

Chief Pleas

The Court of Chief Pleas has no judicial function, and is not known ever to have had one. It is first recorded by name in a document that seems to date from the twelve-seventies,[2] and though no details of its constitution or business at that time are indicated, later records reveal a Court that was held three times a year, after Michaelmas (29 September), after St Maur's day (15 January, often referred to as the session after Christmas), and after Easter. Today the Court sits on the first Monday following these feasts, and did the same at least as far back as the sixteenth century, as regards the Michaelmas and Christmas sessions, although in that era the Easter session convened a fortnight after Easter

---

1. Unless the contrary is made clear, references in this chapter to the Bailiff's presiding over court sessions should be taken to include occasions when the Deputy Bailiff or a Lieutenant-Bailiff supplies his place. These other offices and that of the Jurats are described in the next chapter.
2. De Sausmarez, 1934 39.

Sunday.[3] Chief Pleas traditionally was attended by the *Cour en Corps*, the Law Officers of the Crown, the Advocates, and those manorial *Seigneurs* and *Bordiers* owing suit of court.[4] An Ordinance of 1801 obliged a Constable from each parish to attend also. Historically, the Court witnessed the Greffier administering a roll-call of its members and officers, made and renewed Ordinances (especially after Michaelmas), and, by a procedure known as the *affeurement des rentes*, set the arrear monetary value of property *rentes* paid in kind (also after Michaelmas). Dinner followed.[5] The Royal Court's terms followed each session of Chief Pleas, with, from 1608 at the latest, four Jurats specially assigned to each of the three terms.[6]

Chief Pleas' legislative powers were removed in 1948, and the *affeurement des rentes* had been abolished by an Order in Council of 1927, leaving activity today very limited. The roll-call of members, officers, and certain Crown tenants does continue, although *Bordiers* were excused attendance in 1857, and Advocates and Parish Constables are now obliged to be present only annually, at Chief Pleas after Michaelmas, at which the Lieutenant-Governor sometimes is also present. This session is followed by a service at St Peter Port Church, and, in the evening, the traditional dinner, which is hosted by Her Majesty's Receiver General for certain members and officers of the Court, those private Seigneurs owing suit of court, and the senior Constables of the parishes. The business of Chief Pleas after Michaelmas – usually disposed of within half an hour – involves receiving reports concerning the state of the fencing of quarries from the Constables of each parish, under the *Ordonnance ayant rapport à l'inspection de carrières*, 1932, and from the relevant authorities concerning the renewal of licences of public halls, under the *Loi ayant rapport aux licences pour*

---

3. Commission 1579, 1579 f. 12r.

4. For a full treatment of *bordiers* and their *bordage* tenures, both in Guernsey and elsewhere, see Aubin, 1984. The seigneurial régime has not been so comprehensively examined, but see de Guerin, 1909 i, and Ewen, 1961.

5. Ogier, 2000. Chief Pleas dinners are first recorded in the late thirteenth century, though they quite possibly predated that time. After 1952 the dinner was no longer given three times a year, but annually.

6. The Royal Court's modern calendar continues to provide for three terms, still reckoning from Chief Pleas, but is now organised in four quarters: Christmas, spring, summer, and Michaelmas, for the reason that the responsibilities of the Jurats are shared out on a quarterly rather than a termly basis, with a provision that three Jurats are each on duty for three months of the year.

les salles publiques, 1914, and premises storing explosives, under the *Loi relative aux explosifs*, 1905, as amended. Chief Pleas after Michaelmas also sees the presentation by the Law Officers of the Crown of reports for registration, prepared by the States' Treasury and Resources Department, concerning charitable funds administered by the Royal Court. The session after Christmas receives a report on the state of controlled water courses, due under the *Loi relative aux douits*, 1936, and renews aerodrome licences, in accordance with The Air Navigation Order 1980 as extended to Guernsey under The Air Navigation (Guernsey) Order 1981. Chief Pleas after Easter has no formal business of any similar sort.

In view of the diminution in the business of Chief Pleas, on the recommendation of Her Majesty's Procureur, who had consulted with the Royal Court, and obtained the concurrence of the Policy Council, the States on 29 September 2004 – Michaelmas itself, by coincidence – approved a *Projet de Loi* entitled *The Court of Chief Pleas (Guernsey) Law*, 2004, to provide that the sessions of Chief Pleas after Christmas and after Easter need not be held (though they may be if necessary), and that the manorial tenants should be relieved of their obligation of suit of court on those occasions.

The main business of the Full Court

The Full Court traditionally had no original civil jurisdiction other than in certain administrative matters, such as licensing premises selling liquor, or where hazardous activities went on. It was however a court of appeal, and until 1964, when exercising its civil jurisdiction to review decisions of the Ordinary Court, the Full Court was known as the *Cour des Jugements et Records*.[7] In that year, this jurisdiction was transferred

---

7.   *Plaids des Jugements* are first recorded in 1323, when they were held fortnightly, or at least monthly (Havet, 1878 139–40). By the sixteenth century the *Cour des Jugements et Records* met as necessary, in order to review the decisions of all the Royal Court's lower divisions (Commission 1579, 1579 19r, shows the *Cour des Jugements et Records* operating just such a review function at that date). In its powers of review, which made it until 1964 the forum for appeals from judgments of the Ordinary Division of the Royal Court and, today, under the style of the Royal Court sitting as a Full Court, as a court dealing with appeals from the courts of Alderney and Sark, *requêtes civile* (though these are usually dealt with by the Bailiff sitting alone, technically he does so as the sole judge of law in the Full Court) and (under legislation) certain administrative decisions, the *Cour des Jugements et*

to the Guernsey Court of Appeal. The Full Court also exercised, and in this case continues to exercise, the criminal jurisdiction *grand criminel*, dealing with more serious criminal matters on indictment.

The Full Court's remit has expanded considerably, and now twelve weeks a year are assigned in the Court calendar for the transaction of its business. The present activities of the Full Court can be summarised as follows:

(a) Licensing. Taverns were licensed and regulated in the sixteenth century, and probably earlier (assizes of wine and beer were levied in medieval times, and these may also be thought to be a form of licensing)[8] and today the Royal Court's licensing function principally involves permissions for the *al fresco* sale and supply of intoxicating liquor, (the Ordinary Court generally deals with other liquor licence applications). Other activities which concern the Court are the approval of dates upon which motor racing activities can be conducted, at various locations, permitting the installation of bread ovens within the boundaries of St Peter Port, the approval of applications to raise parochial taxes, the licensing of public halls, and the custody of explosives etc.

(b) Criminal matters. The Full Court's original criminal jurisdiction exists in respect of all indictable offences committed anywhere in the Bailiwick, although this is limited to trial in cases of treason, or assaulting the Bailiff or a Jurat when about his or her duties, with sentence reserved to the Crown (a like limitation in respect of false coining, mentioned in the *Précepte d'Assize* of 1441 and elsewhere, was removed by the *Currency Offences (Guernsey) Law*, 1950). The Full Court also has jurisdiction in offences that are not necessarily indictable, but considered by the Magistrate's Court to be beyond its judicial competence or sentencing powers. The Full Court in practice deals with serious criminal offences

---

Records seems to have taken on the one-time review powers of the Assizes, once these were discontinued after 1331 (Cf. De Sausmarez, 1934 145, 149). Until abolition by Order in Council of 13 May 1823 (registered in Guernsey 28 June 1823) appeal from decisions of the Ordinary Court had in certain circumstances been possible to an intermediate division of the Royal Court, sitting as a *Cour d'appel devant plus de Jurés*, on which see Commission 1815, 1823 10–11.

8. Ogier, 1996 129; Le Patourel, 1937 82.

attracting heavy fines or imprisonment for a period in excess of one year, although persons charged in the Magistrate's Court with an offence, other than assault, which might attract a prison sentence of more than three months may also elect to be tried by it. As part of its criminal jurisdiction the Court also hears appeals in criminal matters in respect of conviction (where the Bailiff sits alone) and sentence (where the Bailiff sits with the Jurats) from the Magistrate's Court, and courts which have dealt with summary matters arising in Alderney and Sark.

(c) Administrative appeals. Quite apart from the developing jurisdiction of the Royal Court to judicially review decisions of States' Departments and Committees and other public bodies, a number of laws specifically provide a right of civil appeal from a decision of a States' Department or other body to the Royal Court sitting as a Full Court. In recent years this jurisdiction has frequently been exercised in respect of decisions of the former Island Development Committee and the former States Housing Authority, and there have been a number of decisions of the Royal Court and the Court of Appeal delimiting judicial powers. Most significantly, the division between matters of law, which are for the Bailiff alone to decide (such as whether or not a decision is *ultra vires*, or unreasonable, in what is known as the 'Wednesbury' sense) and which are unreasonable applying the broader test, which are matters for the Jurats, have been defined.

The Royal Court sitting as the Ordinary Court

As stated above, a minimum of two Jurats and the Bailiff serve the Ordinary Court, although when it sits in sessions of *Plaids d'Héritage*,[9] dealing with the attachment of realty, at least three Jurats sit. More commonly, the business of the Ordinary Court is in the nature of *Plaids de Meubles*. These latter sessions, dealing with chattels, debts, and transgressions, are not mentioned before 1323, when they took place weekly.[10] *Plaids des Meubles' petit criminel* jurisdiction, exercised, under

---

9. A division first mentioned *c*. 1270, when it assembled fortnightly: De Sausmarez, 1934 39. For its later history, see Havet, 1878 135–36.
10. Havet, 1878 137. The statement of Guernsey law and procedures annexed to the report of the Royal Commissioners of 1579 describes what is clearly the *Cour des*

the style of the 'Police Court', by the Ordinary Court in lesser criminal offences was effectively transferred by the *Loi ayant rapport à l'institution d'un Magistrat en Police Correctionelle et pour les recouvrement de menus dettes*, 1925, to a newly instituted Magistrate's Court, though the Ordinary Court retained a concurrent jurisdiction. *The Magistrate's Court (Guernsey) Law,* 1954, abolished the jurisdiction in criminal matters of the Ordinary Court sitting as a Police Court, save in respect of Alderney and Sark in cases where the trial of offences by, or sentencing powers of, their respective courts are beyond their competences. The Ordinary Court will hear such cases, provided the charge is not so serious as to require trial before the Full Court. The Ordinary Court has assumed the functions of now dormant divisions such as *Namps*[11] and *Amirauté*,[12] and it retains original jurisdiction in all civil suits, though in causes where damages or debts claimed are less than £2,500, its jurisdiction is concurrent with that of the Magistrate's Court. The Ordinary Court also hears appeals from the Magistrate's Court in certain civil matters.

Until fairly recently the Ordinary Court assembled weekly, often with a fuller complement than two Jurats and the Bailiff, but now sits

---

Meubles as an extraordinary court, meeting on Wednesdays and Saturdays, under the Bailiff and two Jurats, and dealing with mobiliary and other matters, under the style of *Oeuvres de Marée*. This phrase usually refers to regular works of maintenance to marine vessels, undertaken at low tides. Here, presumably, it is used in a metaphoric sense to refer to a court performing a function that was necessary and routine (Commission 1579, 1579 21v).

11. *Plaids de Namps*, dealing with the distraint of goods secured by legal instrument, are first mentioned in a document of 1393 (Lenfestey, 1978 59). In the later sixteenth century the Royal Court met as *la Cour des tenus de Nampts,* fortnightly, on Mondays (Devyck, 1583; Commission 1579, 1579; Tramallier, 1715). The records of *Plaids de Namps* do not continue as a separate series after 1708.

12. The *extente* of 1331 refers to a Strangers' Court, which would meet daily if necessary, to deal with disputes involving foreigners, although this is done in words that leave it unclear whether these sessions were distinguished from *Plaids de Meubles* other than in respect of the times they were kept. The Strangers' Court anticipated the creation of the Royal Court division *Amirauté*, offering justice in mercantile matters, the registers of which date from 1653. In 1591 the Privy Council had expressed its displeasure at the Court's unauthorised interference in admiralty matters, instructing that it should forbear from such in future (Dasent, 1900 427–8) – but perhaps the relative freedom of the Republican era emboldened the Court to rename as *Amirauté* the long-standing special Strangers' sessions, of which there is evidence of 1583 of continuance (Devyck, 1583). The division's registers indicate that the Royal Court last convened in an *Amirauté* session in 1968.

approximately every two to three weeks, to deal with business such as guardianships, adoptions (*in camera*), company liquidations, evictions, *terres mises à l'amende* applications,[13] and claims for debt where wage arrests are sought. Trials of actions before Jurats are dealt with on specially appointed days for each matter. The Bailiff alone still sits weekly, firstly to deal with non contentious matters, which no longer require the attendance of Advocates before the Court, and secondly to deal with other matters of a procedural and non contentious nature which require a hearing in open court (perhaps because opposition has to be called) yet do not require the participation of the Jurats. Following this weekly sitting the Bailiff usually continues sitting alone in Chambers to deal with interlocutory business and matters requiring directions, a function that is becoming more involved as the Court develops the principles of case management and active judicial control of litigation. Injunctions are also Ordinary Court matters, and are also usually dealt with by the Bailiff sitting alone, as the need arises. Contrastingly, the Ordinary Court business in the Contract Court and Liquor Licence Extension Court that follows it is usually done under the presidency of a Lieutenant-Bailiff appointed from the bench of Jurats.

The Royal Court sitting as the Contract Court

The Ordinary Division of the Royal Court also sits twice-weekly as the Contract Court (often, though too narrowly, called the 'Conveyancing Court'). At least two Jurats, and more usually four, assist the Lieutenant-Bailiff who presides over the Court, attesting transactions such as conveyances of real property, agreements concerning rights in realty, divisions of estates (*partages*), consents to registered charges equivalent to mortgages (bonds), and the completion of documents such as deeds poll, and marriage contracts, and the execution of wills of realty, all of which are thereupon susceptible to registration with the Greffe (although in the case of wills only following the death of the testator).[14]

---

13. Areas of *terres mises à l'amende* may be designated by the Court in order to prevent people who have no right to do so from passing over them. The relevant Ordinances are dated 16 January 1786 and 29 October 1938, as amended.
14. Although the Royal Court has sought the registration of all contracts, for example by an Ordinance of 3 October 1631, and encouraged the registration of

The Matrimonial Causes Division

The Matrimonial Causes Division of the Royal Court was established by *The Matrimonial Causes Law (Guernsey)* 1939. It comprises the Bailiff, sitting alone, or with four Jurats. An amendment of 1946 allowed for the appointment of a legally qualified commissioner as the Judge in Matrimonial Causes, although presently all the Royal Court matrimonial judges hold office as Lieutenant-Bailiffs rather than being appointed commissioners. The 1939 Law, as amended, gives the Division original jurisdiction in matters of divorce, judicial separation, annulments and dissolutions of marriages, and contentious judicial separations. Whilst the Ordinary Court has concurrent jurisdiction in pronouncing and sanctioning the terms of judicial separations by consent, in practice it is the Matrimonial Causes Division that deals with these.

The Magistrate's Court

A Law of 1925 first instituted the Magistrate's Court and the current *Magistrate's Court (Guernsey) Law*, 1954, as amended, gives the Magistrate summary jurisdiction in criminal cases liable to attract a sentence of up to twelve months' imprisonment and/or a fine of five thousand pounds, save where a law specifically provides for a higher maximum penalty, for example relating to fishery offences.[15] The Magistrate also conducts committal proceedings in respect of cases proposed for trial on indictment before the Royal Court, establishing whether there is a case to answer. In practice cases will be sent to the Royal Court for trial (a) where the Magistrate's Court has no jurisdiction to try them, in matters of treason, homicide, rape, robbery, piracy, or perjury, or incitement, conspiracy, or attempting to commit,

---

partages on the Greffe records (eg. by Ordinance of 30 April 1832), in accordance with the Norman legal maxim 'le mort saisit le vif' registration of the latter appears not strictly to be necessary; a *partage* merely distributing an estate between inheritors (or *parceners*) after title has passed, and thus doing no more than evidence an agreement: Cf. Pothier, 1821 244. This interesting observation notwithstanding, *partages* made today are invariably registered upon the records of the Royal Court. The Greffe's property register was established by Ordinance of the Royal Court of 4 October 1563. It is extant, though fragmentarily in its early pages, from 1567.

15.   In 2004 a second stipendiary post, exercising all the powers of the Magistrate as defined in the 1954 law, as amended, was created, with the title 'Assistant Magistrate'.

or aiding and abetting the commission of such offences. These are heard (though not in the case of treason sentenced) by the Royal Court, (b) where the Law Officers or the Magistrate consider that the sentencing powers of the Magistrate's Court are inadequate, having regard to the seriousness of the offence, (c) on the election of the accused or the Law Officers, if the maximum sentence exceeds three months, save that the defendant has no such power in cases of assault, or (d) in cases brought under Section 1(2) of *The Criminal Damage (Bailiwick of Guernsey) Law*, 1983, Section 13 of which denies the Magistrate jurisdiction in matters of the destruction or damage of property where life may be endangered, for example by arson.

The Magistrate's Court has jurisdiction in civil matters where the sum in dispute does not exceed £2,500 ('petty debts') and also in respect of some matrimonial cases, in matters of separation, maintenance, affiliation, and the custody of children, principally under the *Domestic Proceedings and Magistrate's Court (Guernsey) Law*, 1988, as amended. Section three of *The Magistrate's Court (Guernsey) Law*, 1954, as substituted by *The Magistrate's Court and Miscellaneous Reforms (Guernsey) Law*, 1996, provides that the Magistrate should be a Guernsey or Jersey Advocate, or United Kingdom barrister or solicitor, of at least five years' standing. The Law of 1925 that instituted the Magistrate's Court transferred from the Royal Court to the Magistrate jurisdiction to hold inquests. These are held at the direction of the Law Officers of the Crown, who are responsible for the preliminary investigations into all deaths where the deceased may have met an unnatural or violent end, or died in prison, or in other circumstances where for some reason a doctor cannot sign a death certificate.

The Juvenile Court

The Juvenile Court is part of the Magistrate's Court. As presently constituted it is the creation of *The Juvenile Court (Guernsey) Law*, 1989. The Magistrate, as chairman, and two members, selected from the Juvenile Court Panel appointed by the Royal Court sitting as a Full Court, serve it. The Juvenile Court must include at least one man and one woman, save that in certain circumstances the Magistrate will sit alone. The Court deals with juveniles (ie. those under seventeen years of age) who are charged with offences, or in need of care, protection or control under *The Children and Young Persons (Guernsey) Law*, 1967, as amended, or who should be secured to attend school regularly as provided for by *The Education (Guernsey) Law*, 1970.

The Guernsey Court of Appeal

Following a resolution of 1960 the States petitioned for the revocation of the Court of Appeal (Channel Islands) Order 1949, which had not taken effect, because it had contemplated a single Court of Appeal for Guernsey and Jersey, and difficulties had been foreseen. It was therefore resolved that there should be separate Courts for each of the Bailiwicks. The States of Guernsey submitted their own *Projet de Loi* entitled *The Court of Appeal (Guernsey) Law*, 1961. Duly sanctioned, the Law's terms were brought into force on 4 June 1964, by Ordinance. The Bailiff is a judge *ex officio* and the Court's president. In practice, the Court, comprising 'outside' judges, convenes four times a year, or as need requires, and the Bailiff has tended only to sit on an *ad hoc* basis, as some of his own decisions may be subject to appeal. The ordinary judges, who may be drawn from the Commonwealth judiciary or the British or Channel Island bars, and who are often eminent Queen's Counsel, are appointed by Her Majesty, holding office during good behaviour, usually until the age of seventy years, which may be specially extended, though this has happened only rarely. The quorum is usually three judges, although a single judge may sit on applications of a procedural nature, and sometimes the judges will sit as a bench of five, in order to consider several appeals and set guidelines. Appeals are heard in Guernsey, save when a judge is sitting alone, when any location is permitted. Questions are determined by majority. Her Majesty's Greffier, Sheriff, and Sergeant are the Guernsey Court of Appeal's executive officers, and Guernsey Advocates have the sole right to practise before it. The Bailiffs of Guernsey and Jersey are usually appointed judges in the Court of Appeal of each other's islands and regularly sit as such.

In 1964 the Guernsey Court of Appeal assumed the powers, in Civil matters, of the Royal Court constituted as the *Cour des Jugements et Records*, within the limits set out in Section 15 of *The Court of Appeal (Guernsey) Law*, 1961.[16] Permission to appeal to the Privy Council from

---

16. These limits have been interpreted judicially not only by the Court of Appeal's judgment of 14 December 1998 in *Bassington Limited and others v H.M. Procureur,*

the Court of Appeal's decisions, where the value of the matter in dispute is less than five hundred pounds, can only be obtained by special leave of Her Majesty in Council, or by leave of the Court itself.

Before 1964, when *The Court of Appeal (Guernsey) Law*, 1961, was brought into full effect, criminal appeals from the Royal Court sitting as a Full Court could only proceed, with special leave, to the Judicial Committee of the Privy Council. The Law established the Guernsey Court of Appeal (Criminal Division) which hears appeals against conviction by the Royal Court, sitting as a Full Court, where the ground of appeal involves a question of law alone or, with leave and certification, mixed questions, or questions of fact alone. The Court of Appeal will also, on leave, hear appeals against sentence, unless the penalty is fixed by legislation. It may allow appeals, dismiss them, quash criminal sentences, or diminish or increase them. The Law Officers of the Crown, or Advocates of their Chambers, appear for the Crown before the Court of Appeal in all such circumstances.

The Judicial Committee of the Privy Council

The Judicial Committee of the Privy Council is generally the court of last resort in appeals from the judgments of Bailiwick Courts. It is served by the Lord Chancellor and past Lords Chancellor, Lords of Appeal in Ordinary (some of whom are also the Law Lords in the House of Lords, or other Lords of Appeal) and other Privy Councillors with distinguished judicial service in the United Kingdom or elsewhere in the Commonwealth. The Lords of Appeal in Ordinary undertake most of the work. The quorum is three, though usually five judges will sit. All, save the Lord Chancellor, are required to be less than seventy-five years of age.[17]

---

cited above, but also by its judgment of 20 September 2002, in the matter of *The Island Development Committee v Portholme Properties Limited*, in which the Court asserted a jurisdiction in appeals from Full Court decisions made under the terms of *The Island Development (Guernsey) Law*, 1966, as amended.

17. Although the Parliamentary Secretary, Department for Constitutional Affairs, stated in a House of Commons' written answer of 17 July 2003 that Her Majesty's Government is not proposing any change in the status of the Judicial Committee as a forum for appeal for independent jurisdictions, and that members of the proposed Supreme Court would be appointed to it, quite where matters stand after the House of Lords' reference on 8 March 2004 to a special select committee of the Constitutional Reform Bill (which would have abolished the office of Lord

The powers of the Judicial Committee ultimately derive from the Royal Prerogative, via the Medieval *Curia Regis*, on the principle that the sovereign (at one period the Duke of Normandy) is the fount of justice, with authority to remedy the errors of, and grievances against, his or her Courts. Such a power functioned with the advice of the king's Council, which exercised appellate jurisdiction in respect of the Channel Islands from an early date, including, perhaps, the period when they were part of the Angevin Empire.[18] By 1540, the Council had been refined and reorganised to the extent that the Privy Council proper may be identified.[19] From 1696, the Appeals Committee of the Privy Council heard appeals, and, in 1833, the modern Judicial Committee of the Privy Council was created.[20] Judgments still reflect the prerogative aspect of the Council's function, taking the form of advice of the Judicial Committee to the Queen that she should follow a particular course in the matter appealed.[21] The law that the Committee applies in Guernsey cases is, naturally, the law of Guernsey.

Modern authorities have cited an Order in Council of 1495 as establishing that appeals from Jersey should be heard exclusively by the King in Council, and inferred that this Order was observed in respect of all the Channel Islands.[22] I have traced no such clear injunction. It only appears that an Order of 17 June 1495 stated that cases of treason suspected or arising in Jersey should be reserved solely to the king and his Council for examination and determination. An associated direction, of Henry VII, of 3 November 1494, remitted any complaints of Governors against the administration of justice in Jersey to the Council's cognisance.[23] Later decrees do, however, offer evidence that, if the extent of the Council's appellate jurisdiction may not have been as clearly defined in the fifteenth century as some recent authors have suggested, it certainly was distinct in the sixteenth. An Order was made on 22 June 1565 by which the Privy Council, after receiving the opinion of the

---

Chancellor, and established a Supreme Court) is at present unclear. It should be added that the present Lord Chancellor has as a matter of policy declined to sit in a judicial capacity.

18. Howell, 1979 3–4.
19. Elton, 1982 91.
20. Howell, 1979 7.
21. Cf. Maitland, 1908 463.
22. E.g. Howell, 1979 5; Baker, 1990 34.
23. Prison Board, 1894 app. ii 179–93.

English Solicitor-General and the Lords Chief Justice, confirmed that no appeals from the Channel Islands '… should be made from any sentence in judgment given in the same isles hither, but only according to the words of their charters, *au Roi et son Conseil*, which agrees, as Sir Hugh Powlet [the Governor of Jersey] alleges, with such order and form as has heretofore been accustomed …'.[24] That this was indeed the 'accustomed' procedure before 1565 is suggested by Elizabeth I's charter of 1560, which, after extensive reference to the laws, customs, and rights of the Bailiwick, saved under the prerogative power 'to the aforesaid islanders, and others dwelling or being in the said islands, a right to appeal in all cases reserved to our cognisance and consideration by the laws and customs of the said island; but in no other case'.[25]

Rules for appeals from Guernsey were set out in detail in an Order in Council of 9 October 1580.[26] This Order, parts of which were reiterated and occasionally varied by further Orders over the years, confirmed the inhabitants' right to appeal to the Council, providing this was asserted within fifteen days of the judgment complained of, and excepting appeals, in 'any cause criminal or of correction', against the execution of Ordinances made at Chief Pleas, or against judgments following *Clameurs de Haro*.[27] Appeals in mobiliary matters where less than ten pounds were in dispute were not to be entertained, nor were appeals to be made from interim judgments. The Order of 1580 also required, subject to certain conditions, that appeals should be prosecuted and concluded within a year and a day of sentence, sureties be supplied, and undertakings for costs given. The Royal Court was enjoined to supply proper records of proceedings.

Appeals to the Privy Council are presently governed by the Judicial Committee (General Appellate Jurisdiction) Rules Order 1982, registered in Guernsey on 17 May 1983, as amended.[28] Current Privy Council documentation states that the other principal items of legislation relating

---

24.   Dasent, 1893 224. The word 'alleges' in this passage is used in the archaic sense of a declaration of the law.

25.   Thornton, 2004 93, translated from the Latin.

26.   Commission 1846, 1848 313.

27.   The *Clameur d'Haro* is a means, involving some ceremony, of obtaining an injunction and seeking satisfaction in respect of interference with the *clamant*'s property: see Sherwill, 1947; Carey, 1991; Pissard, 1911.

28.   On the general jurisdiction of the Judicial Committee, see Roberts-Wray, 1966 434–45.

to the Judicial Committee and its proceedings with regard to Guernsey are two Orders in Council of 13 May 1823 and 15 July 1835. The former of these confined appeals to the Council to cases where the value of the object in dispute, if realty, amounted to more than ten pounds annually, and, if personalty, to two hundred pounds Sterling, and required that appeals should be prosecuted within six months of the judgment challenged. The second Order decreed that appeals from the Channel Islands should be subject to the same rules from time to time in force for the Colonies as to setting down for hearing and being heard, and that respondents should appear before the Council within forty days of being summoned to do so.

It should be added that other legislation has further modified the financial qualifications, including Section 16 of *The Court of Appeal (Guernsey) Law*, 1961, which provides that, unless with the special leave of either forum, no appeal from the Court of Appeal to the Judicial Committee of the Privy Council lies, except where the matter in dispute equals or exceeds £500. In the spirit of the Order of 1580, criminal appeals are not usually admitted, although they have been so on occasion, by the Council's special leave. The terms of an Order in Council dated 11 July 1734, following an appeal by James Perchard from a Royal Court judgment in an action of *Clameur de Haro*, suggest that in this area also the rules of 1580 have been modified. Overall, the modern Judicial Committee has discretion in relation to decisions of the Guernsey Courts, and experience shows that it exercises this discretion sparingly.[29]

Postscript: subordinate manorial courts

In the Medieval and Early Modern periods, manorial courts served several localities. These employed various numbers of *Vavasseurs* (the jurymen) under the presidency of a *Sénéchal*. Their main activities related to debt recovery, dealing with straying animals,[30] and appointing manorial officers.[31] The courts had no criminal jurisdiction and a right of

---

29.   Cf. Gahan, 1963 156–57.
30.   Cf. Commission 1607, 1814 59.
31.   A Royal Court judgment of 30 June 1705 barred the court of Fief St Michel, and by implication all other manorial courts, from in future administering oaths to guardians.

appeal to the Royal Court against their judgments existed. The courts of Fiefs St Michel and le Comte possessed their own seals, and, imitating the Royal Court, employed these to validate contracts. Over the centuries, such functions were whittled away. The court of Fief le Comte ceased passing contracts *c*. 1810, and in 1861 the court of Fief St Michel was wholly suppressed by law.[32] *The Feudal Dues (Guernsey) Law*, 1980 abolished the private collection of manorial dues. The lands of the fiefs and in certain cases financial interests do survive, and a couple of courts still find it necessary to meet, whether on administrative matters, or for ceremonial reasons, or a combination of the both. Certain *Seigneurs* (and *Dames*) are still obliged to answer for their fiefs before the Royal Court at Chief Pleas, where also one or another of the Law Officers of the Crown reminds the Court of Her Majesty's interest in respect of appropriated Crown fiefs, and of the Bailiff's in respect of Fief de Blanchelande, of which he is *ex officio* seigneur, under the terms of a will of realty registered 1 September 1945.

32.   de Guérin, 1909 i 71, 72. This says that the court of Fief le Comte 'retained its jurisdiction up to 1775, when it was suppressed by Bailiff William Le Marchant'. Notwithstanding Le Marchant's intentions in that regard a Privy Council direction of 1776 in fact allowed for the manorial court's continuance (de Sausmarez, 1965 720, Tupper, 1876 409–10). The *c*. 1810 date, above, is supplied by personal information from the present Seigneur of Fief le Comte.

6. The Bailiff and other Officers of and about the Royal Court

The Bailiff

The Bailiff is Guernsey's leading citizen and representative in non-political matters, with functions embracing judicial and civic duties, and a more limited but important parliamentary role.[1]

The office had become distinct from that of sub-warden in the early fourteenth century, with the title *ballivus* being reserved for the officer

---

1. Guernsey's Bailiffs 1340-present are: 1340–1357, Jean de Lande; 1357–1384, Jean le Marchant; 1384–1387, Jean Nicholas; 1387–1412, Gervaise de Clermont; 1412–1433, James Coquerel; 1433–1446, Thomas de la Cour; 1446–1447, Jean Henry; 1447–1466, Guillaume Cartier; 1467–1470, Thomas de la Cour; 1470–1480, Pierre de Beauvoir; 1480–1481, Edmond de Cheyney; 1481–1482, Nicholas Fouaschin; 1482–1499, Jean Blondel; 1499–1511, Jean Martin; 1511–1538, James Guille; 1538–1545, Thomas Compton; 1545–1549, Jean Herivel; 1549–1562, Helier Gosselin; 1563–1571, Thomas Compton; 1572–1581, Guillaume Beauvoir; 1581–1587, Thomas Wigmore; 1588–1600, Louis Devyck; 1601–1631, Amice de Carteret; 1631–1643, Jean de Quetteville; (1643–1644, Jean Bonamy, *juge délégué*); (1644, Jacques Guille, *juge délégué*); 1644–1646, Pierre de Beauvoir; (1647, Jean Carey, *juge délégué*); 1647–1650, Pierre du Beauvoir; (1650–1652, Jean Bonamy, *juge délégué*); (1652, Jacques Guille, *juge délégué*); 1652–1653, Pierre du Beauvoir; (between September 1653 and February 1656 the jurats filled the office by monthly rotation); 1656–1660, Pierre de Beauvoir; (1660–1661, Josué Gosselin *juge délégué*); 1661–1674, Amias Andros; 1674–1714, Sir Edmund Andros; 1714–1728, Jean de Sausmarez; 1728–1752, Joshua Le Marchant; 1752–1758, Eleazar Le Marchant; 1758–1771, Samuel Bonamy; 1771–1800, William Le Marchant; 1800–1810, Robert Porret Le Marchant; 1810–1821, Sir Peter de Havilland; 1821–1842, Daniel de Lisle Brock; 1843–1845, John Guille; 1845–1883, Sir Peter Stafford Carey; 1883–1884, Jean de Havilland Utermarck; 1884–1895, Sir Edgar MacCulloch; 1895–1902, Sir Thomas Godfrey Carey; 1902–1908, Sir Henry Alexander Giffard; 1908–1915, Sir William Carey; 1915–1922, Sir Edward Chepmell Ozanne; 1922–1929, Sir Havilland Walter de Sausmarez, bart; 1929–1935, Arthur William Bell; 1935–1946, Sir Victor Gosselin Carey; 1946–1960, Sir Ambrose James Sherwill; 1960–1973, Sir William Henry Arnold; 1973–1982, Sir John Henry Loveridge; 1982–1992, Sir Charles Keith Frossard; 1992–1999, Sir Graham Martyn Dorey; 1999- Sir de Vic Graham Carey. (Sources: Lenfestey, 1978 151, Berry, 1815 195–97, and almanacs for the period 1821-present).

who presided over the Royal Court, hence assuming responsibilities for judicial duties that had formally been assigned by the king to a succession of Wardens in the aftermath of the loss of Normandy in 1204.[2] Though in the Medieval period often appointed by the Warden, the Bailiff might also be appointed by the king, and his office in a few decades became largely independent of the former.[3] Bailiffs were required to be resident in Guernsey, and whilst the Jurats had the sole power to render judgments, he directed them, and announced their verdicts, and as Professor Le Patourel wrote, he '... also became the natural leader of any insular impatience with the Warden's administration'.[4] The Bailiff has also since the early fourteenth century been the keeper of the official seal of the Bailiwick, though this may only be used in the presence of two Jurats.[5]

For a long period, Bailiffs were usually appointed from the bench of Jurats. The last such was Sir Henry Alexander Giffard, QC, (1838–1927) a Jurat 1899–1902 and Bailiff 1902–08. Giffard had retired to his native island after a notable career at the English Bar. The last lay Bailiff appointed was Sir Edgar MacCulloch (1808–96) a Jurat 1844–84 and Bailiff 1884–95. Since MacCulloch's time, all Bailiffs have been qualified lawyers, often having first served as H.M. Procureur, and as Deputy Bailiff, since the creation of the latter office in 1969.

Today, the Bailiff and Deputy Bailiff of Guernsey are appointed by the sovereign by letters patent under the Great Seal, holding office during Her Majesty's pleasure. The letters patent throughout the twentieth century provided for a retirement age of seventy, but in 1999 this was reduced to sixty-five years. The Deputy Bailiff continues the Court's judicial work and discharges the Bailiff's parliamentary duties when the island is without a Bailiff, between appointments, though a *Juge Délégué* (usually the senior Jurat) will preside over the sitting when

---

2. Le Patourel, 1937 47–49, 51. The offices of Warden, Governor (or Captain) and Lieutenant-governor are treated in Chapter nine, below.

3. An Order in Council of 27 May 1674 expressly denied a Governor's claim to appoint the Bailiff, though this apparently was usual until the early part of that century: Havet, 1878 38.

4. Le Patourel, 1937 88–90. Dr Owen cites an example of 1714–27 of an absentee Bailiff and the problems thereanent. He also recounts in connection with that affair a justification for the Governor being debarred from appointing any Bailiff, in order that the relationship should not be one as of patron to client (Owen, 2000 144–45).

5. Le Patourel, 1937 98.

a new Bailiff is robed and sworn into office, at which point the *Juge Délégué* relinquishes office *ipso jure*.

The Bailiff's oath, still taken in French, and administered by the *Juge Délégué*, includes the following words:

> ... that you will well and faithfully and to all your power keep and maintain all the laws, liberties, usages and ancient customs of this island, in concert with the Jurats of this island, and will execute and carry out the inspections,[6] records and judgments made and announced by the said Jurats, and that, if by error or otherwise you shall make any omission or error to the contrary, you shall forthwith amend yourself according to the advice and good opinion of the said Jurats, that you will not seal any documents that are not legal and juridical and that of all sales, obligations, sentences or scheduling of causes (*termes de role*) which shall be made before you, you will give true reports and records ...[7]

Appointments are made following a recommendation by the retiring Bailiff in the case of the appointment of a new Bailiff, and by the Bailiff in the case of a Deputy Bailiff. The Bailiff will invariably have consulted the Jurats and other judges, the Chief Minister and Acting Presiding Officers of the States of Deliberation, and may consult some senior members of the legal profession, as to the relative merits of applicants. He will also have conferred with the Lieutenant-Governor, before transmitting a recommendation to the latter for conveyance to the Department for Constitutional Affairs, which will then make a recommendation to Her Majesty the Queen.

Following the removal in 1964 of the Jurats' competence in the Royal Court as sole judges of law, the Bailiff, or Deputy Bailiff, or sometimes a Lieutenant-Bailiff, now sits alone in judgment where matters of fact are not at issue, and is solely responsible for questions not only of law, but also of procedure and costs. When presiding with Jurats, he or she directs them on questions of law, identifies the facts at issue, and

---

6. This word – *regards* in the original – seems to refer to what are now called *vues de justice*, when the Court will transport itself beyond its usual seat, the better to understand a matter under consideration.

7. Le Cerf, 1863 285 supplies the oath in the words still sworn, save that line 14 of the published version misprints '... erreur *et* autrement ...' for '... erreur *ou* autrement', and also, of course, the name of the reigning monarch has changed.

summarises what should be considered in their deliberations. Directions are given in open court and 'on the record'. As Crown appointees, the Bailiff and Deputy Bailiff cannot be removed for political reasons, nor their judicial functions interfered with politically.

The Bailiff is also *ex officio* President of the Guernsey Court of Appeal. He does not preside routinely in this capacity other than as a single judge to deal with interim applications, such as applications for leave to appeal from decisions given by other Royal Court judges.

The other main duty of the Bailiff is to act as Presiding Officer of the States of Deliberation, serving as moderator of debate in the assembly, ruling on questions of procedure, and maintaining order. He will also exceptionally (for example in the absence from the assembly of a Law Officer) be invited to advise or caution the assembly on constitutional law and procedure, which requires immediate knowledge of the privileges, rights, and customs of the Bailiwick. In the Bailiff's absence these functions are performed by the Deputy Bailiff, as Deputy Presiding Officer, or, often momentarily, by one of the three Acting Presiding Officers who are nominated by the Bailiff at the start of each four year States' term. He will normally chose the three longest serving members of the assembly to hold that office.

In the States of Deliberation, under the Reform Law of 1948, the Bailiff or his substitute had a casting vote, but now, under Article 1(4) of *The Reform (Guernsey) (Amendment) Law*, 2003, has 'no casting vote, and in the event of an equality of votes he shall (except in the case of an election) declare the proposition lost'. In the case of voting in elections for Presidents and Members of Departments and Chairmen and Members of States' Committees, the Rules of Procedure provide a tie-breaking mechanism involving the casting of lots that must be followed. In meetings of the States of Election, the Presiding Officer does not have a casting vote in the first instance, but in the event of an equality of votes he does, which by law is exercisable by private intimation to scrutineers appointed by the assembly.

Billets d'État, convening meetings of the States, are issued in the Bailiff's name, under the style of Presiding Officer. These contain particulars of the matters to be debated, together with propositions designed to enable the States to make Resolutions. Until recently *Billets* were compiled and produced by the Bailiff's small secretariat under the authority of the Bailiff on receipt of Policy Letters and legislation tendered for inclusion by the Presidents of States' Committees. In 2004 this responsibility for compilation and production was transferred to the new Policy Council. The Chief Minister and the Policy Council's secretariat will now confer with the Bailiff on the volume of business to be included in a *Billet d'État*, if it is estimated that the proposed business may not readily be dealt with within the time allocated to sessions. The Presiding Officer is at liberty to comment on the wording of the propositions if there is any lack of clarity. There will also be consultation with the Presiding Officer if the Policy Council or the signatories to a *requête* require that an urgent additional meeting of the States should be convened by the Presiding Officer.

On appointment, as provided for in Lieutenant-Governors' warrants, the Bailiff is sworn-in as Deputy Lieutenant-Governor, in order to serve in the Lieutenant-Governor's place in his absence or if for any other cause he is unable to act. The Deputy Bailiff is similarly sworn to serve in the absence of both, and the senior Jurat in case all three are absent or for some cause unable to act. The time spent in discharging this deputising role has declined in recent times in view of technological advances, allowing a Lieutenant-Governor absent from the Bailiwick to deal with issues at a distance.

Over recent decades, the Bailiff's role in Guernsey's administration has diminished considerably, and the last few remnants, namely presidency of the former Rules of Procedure Committee, the Legislation Committee, the Appointments Board, and the Emergency Council, have been transferred to Departments and Committees of the States. At the same time, the number of cases to be determined in the Courts has increased dramatically, forming a more substantial part of his work. Letters from Guernsey for the attention of United Kingdom Government ministers are sent through the formal constitutional channel of the Bailiff's Chambers to the Office of the Lieutenant-Governor for onward transmission, but less formal communications, whether by letter or otherwise, between senior civil servants in Guernsey and the United Kingdom are now routine. Internationally, the Chief Minister, Ministers, the Law Officers, or the Chief Executive of the States of Guernsey will represent Guernsey's interests in discussions or negotiations on matters that are clearly within the province of the Policy Council.

The Bailiff as civic head of the community still represents Guernsey internationally on occasions of a non-political nature, and will on behalf of the people of Guernsey greet and welcome members of the Royal Family and dignitaries visiting the island. His other civic duties within and outside Guernsey are numerous and varied, for example ranging from attending the opening ceremony of the Commonwealth Games to presiding over the Council of the Guille Allès Library, because the constitution of that library drawn up by its founders so provides. The Bailiff and his spouse by convention also accept appointment as patrons of a substantial number of Guernsey charities.

The Deputy Bailiff

The Deputy Bailiff (Guernsey) Law, 1969, created the office of Deputy Bailiff. He is the second senior judicial officer. Whilst protecting the *status quo* with regard to any Acting Presidents of the States (a position now designated 'Acting Presiding Officer') and *Juges Délégué* from time to time in office, the Law provides that the Deputy Bailiff may, amongst other things, with the authority of the Bailiff discharge any of the functions or powers of the Bailiff and that he should exercise the same during the absence or incapacity of the Bailiff or a vacancy. His work is principally judicial but he will from time to time discharge the duty of Deputy Presiding Officer of the States of Deliberation, and sometimes that of acting Lieutenant-Governor, as well as civic duties in the absence of the Bailiff. He ranks second in civic precedence immediately after the Bailiff.

Judicial assistance to the Bailiff

Bailiffs customarily enjoy the power to appoint one or more Lieutenants, who serve for no longer than the duration of office of the Bailiff who appoints them. Historically, for example sometimes in the eighteenth century, Lieutenant-Bailiffs exercised almost all the powers of the Bailiff.[8] These were recruited from the ranks of the Jurats, and today the four senior Jurats are appointed Lieutenant-Bailiffs and preside over the Contract Court and Liquor Licence Extension Court that follows it.

---

8. E.g. see Hocart, 1988 3.

Generally, 'Jurat' Lieutenant-Bailiffs do not nowadays preside over other divisions of the Royal Court except in cases of urgency. On the appointment of a legally qualified Magistrate, it became the practice for Magistrates to be appointed Lieutenant-Bailiffs, although the necessity for this declined on the appointment of a full time Deputy Bailiff in 1969. The increased demands on the time of the Bailiff and his Deputy have led to an increase in appointments of legally qualified Lieutenant-Bailiffs, some resident in Guernsey. The resident Lieutenant-Bailiffs sit frequently whilst the non-resident Lieutenant-Bailiffs sit when the resident judges have a conflict of interest, or when there is a need to cope with any litigation backlog. One of the present Lieutenant-Bailiffs is a specialist judge dealing with disputed legal costs cases.

The Jurats

The Jurats of the Royal Court (known in French as *Jurés*, or sometimes *Jurés Justiciers*) although directed by the Bailiff, traditionally were the sole judges of both law and fact, forming, in Professor Le Patourel's words, 'a bench of "doomsmen" or "judgement finders"', elected for life.[9] They were, and to an extent remain, personifications of the island's legal identity. The bench of Jurats seems not to have been instituted at the date of the earliest recorded mention of the Royal Court of 1179, and in 1248 it was stated that King John had instituted *duodecim coronatores juratos*, in the Islands after the loss of Normandy.[10] In these 'twelve sworn coroners', we perhaps see the Jurats in their nascent form. Indeed, the Jurats' role closely resembled both those of officers serving communes created by John in his other French territories, and also the English office of coroner, created in 1194, and developed by John.[11]

About this period, Jurats may sometimes have physically participated in the apprehension of malefactors.[12] They tended to be drawn from well-to-do local families, and the *Précepte d'Assize* (1441) described the bench as comprising 'twelve of the most notable, impartial, wise, loyal and rich' men of the island (*douze hommez dez plus notablez et discres sages loyaulx*

9. Le Patourel, 1937 91.
10. De Sausmarez, 1934 27.
11. Havet, 1878 ch. 3; Everard and Holt, 2004 158–59.
12. Le Patourel, 1951.

et riches en la dicte ysle).[13] Until well into the eighteenth century, relatively young gentlemen often served in the office, although any requirement for participation in active law enforcement had long gone. Election as a Jurat is regarded as an honour, but today the States of Election tend to value worldly experience, intellect, and integrity, over some of the qualifications that may have influenced selection in the distant past.

The Royal Court of Guernsey (Miscellaneous Reform Provisions) Law, 1950 extended eligibility for the office of Jurat to the Roman Catholic and other faiths, all trades – brewers, for example, were once excluded – and women, though it was not until 1985 that the first woman Jurat was elected. It also provided for a retirement age of seventy years, which may be extended to seventy-five with the Court's agreement, and that upon ceasing to hold office a Jurat 'shall continue to enjoy for the remainder of his life the honours and privileges appertaining to the office ...'. A further provision of the Law, brought in by an Order of the Royal Court of 1964, removed the Jurats' competence as judges of law, the Bailiff being confirmed as the sole judge of law in the Royal Court. No Jurat is allowed concurrently to be a People's Deputy or Douzenier, and a People's Deputy or Douzenier must resign upon election as a Jurat, under Article 1 (5) of *The Reform (Guernsey) (Amendment) Law,* 2003, amending Article 2 of the Reform Law of 1948.

The Jurats' oath involves undertakings to maintain Guernsey's polity (*la république de cette île*) and uphold its laws, liberties, customs, and other legal usages, to serve as required in Court, rendering justice to all, great or small, particularly widows and orphans, not to accept bribes, and to assist in the keeping of accurate records. Two Jurats have to be present at the Bailiff's affixing of the Bailiwick Seal, and only Jurats may attest wills of Guernsey realty completed in the island.

In reaching decisions, the finding of a majority of the Jurats sitting suffices. Usually they retire to the Jurats' room to reach a decision, following the summing-up of the presiding judge in open court. The judge is not present during deliberations, although in the case of an even division between the Jurats, he or she has a casting vote. After the Bench reaches a decision in criminal trials, the senior Jurat reports it in open court, indicating whether it was reached unanimously or, if not, the

---

13.   Ogier, 1990 ii 47.

number who found the defendant guilty or not guilty. Save in cases where a fixed penalty applies, the presiding judge then retires with the Jurats concerning the Court's sentence, giving them guidance on relevant guideline and precedent cases that they ought to take into consideration. The sentence is then stated to the presiding judge, together with any relevant reasons or observations, which is then declared by the judge in open court, with appropriate reasons and remarks.

The Law Officers of the Crown

The Law Officers of the Crown are Her Majesty's Procureur, otherwise known as Her Majesty's Attorney General, and Her Majesty's Comptroller, otherwise known as Her Majesty's Solicitor General. Both hold office during Her Majesty's pleasure by Royal Warrant, subject to retirement at sixty-five years of age. Historically, the Law Officers of the Crown were free to undertake private legal work, but this was abandoned in the case of H.M. Procureur in 1920, and H.M. Comptroller in 1940.[14]

The materially similar oaths of the Law Officers of the Crown include promises to obey the Court and its acts and their execution, to uphold the public interest, to keep and observe the laws, rights, ancient liberties, and usages of Guernsey, and to pursue and defend all Crown interests. Although the Comptroller fills the junior position, he is not accountable to the Procureur, and may hold a different view. The position of H.M. Procureur is distinguishable from the fourteenth century, when a pleader for the king first occurs in the records.[15] The office of H.M. Comptroller, known in French as that of the *Contrôle*, appears not to be so ancient. Although mentioned in 1583 as having existed since the memory of man ran not to the contrary,[16] it is not referred to in the *Précepte d'Assize*, nor in other Medieval documents. On the other hand, although the first known appointment of a Comptroller was that of Nicollas Trohardy in 1554, clearly at that date it was already an established office, and it may be that the post was created in the late fifteenth century. The office was

---

14. An Ordinance of the Royal Court of 30 September 1588 had denied both Law Officers the power to plead for private persons, but this prohibition, if it ever took effect, must have lapsed in later years.
15. Le Patourel, 1937 94.
16. Devyck, 1583 6v.

suspended for practical reasons in 1851, and revived by an Order in Council ten years later.

Both Law Officers of the Crown are non-voting members of the States of Deliberation, where they will speak as appropriate on constitutional and legal issues.[17] They and their professional staff provide legal advice to the States and their Departments and Committees, the Guernsey Financial Services Commission, and other public bodies (though all are free to consult other counsel should they wish to) and on matters of constitutional significance will give advice to parish authorities. They also advise H.M. Greffier, Sheriff, and Sergeant. The Law Officers advise on reports published in *Billets d'État*, and States' Members' amendments and *requêtes*. They draft *Projets de Loi*, Ordinances, Rules of Court and other legal instruments, including contracts for States' land transactions. They represent the States in Guernsey's Courts and also, as necessary, before the Judicial Committee of the Privy Council and the European Courts. They advise the Courts, when requested, as *amici curiæ*. All criminal proceedings are brought in the name of the Law Officers, indeed there is no right to bring a private prosecution. The Law Officers advise on prosecutions conducted by the Police, and, in some criminal matters, they themselves, or, more often in recent years, Advocates of their Chambers (the more senior of whom, with the approval of the Royal Court, are accorded the dignity of 'Crown Advocate') prosecute, and also appear for the prosecution on appeals before the Royal Court, and the Guernsey Court of Appeal. They also obtain confiscation and restraint orders relating to the proceeds of crime, and process requests from outside the Bailiwick seeking assistance in criminal investigations. They and their professional staff conduct civil litigation on behalf of the States, and deal with both administrative and statutory appeals in areas ranging from child care to planning. They also have duties in connection with inquests, cremations, certain hospital admissions, and the needs of children for care and protection. Both Law Officers are *ex officio* the Crown's Proctors in the Ecclesiastical Court. Her Majesty's Procureur is

---

17. Section 1 (5) (b) of *The Reform (Guernsey) Law*, 1948 effectively put an end to the voting rights in the States of Deliberation that the Law Officers of the Crown had enjoyed. Hocart, 1988 130–32 recounts the end. H.M. Procureur had been a voting member from time immemorial. H.M. Comptroller only became a member of, and was given a vote in, the States of Deliberation in 1899, under the *Loi Relative à la Réforme des États de Délibération* of that year. He became a member of the States of Election under the *Loi Relative aux États d'Election*, 1901.

the head of the Guernsey Bar, and, since 1985, has filled the post of Her Majesty's Receiver General. In recent years, the Procureur has also increasingly been involved in advising the States' Advisory and Finance Committee – and now its successors, principally the Policy Council – in connection with relations with bodies as various as United Kingdom Government Departments, the European Union, the Organisation for Economic Co-operation and Development, the Financial Action Task Force, the United Nations, and foreign governments.

Her Majesty's Greffier

Her Majesty's Greffier is Clerk of the Court and Clerk and Registrar of the States. In 1219, a *clerc* to the Warden (or Bailiff) was mentioned. A statement of 1320 that the *clericus curiae domini regis* should be neither a merchant nor taverner clearly associated a clerk, probably the same officer, with the Royal Court.[18] By the sixteenth century the clerk had acquired the name of *Greffier*, and his registry, the *Greffe*. The Greffier holds office during Her Majesty's pleasure by Royal Warrant, subject to retirement at sixty-five years of age. As Clerk of the Royal Court, he is responsible for preparing lists of causes, maintaining records of proceedings, registering judgments, orders, and other records, and drafting Court documents. He has similar responsibilities with regard to the Guernsey Court of Appeal and Magistrate's Court. He registers property transactions, including all conveyances and some leases, and the imposition of charges on realty (including bonds, which are equivalent to mortgages), also assessing duty on these and other documents. The Greffier is registrar of companies, and of patents, designs, and trademarks. He administers maintenance and affiliation orders. He is also, under an Ordinance of the Royal Court sanctioned by an Order in Council of 1840, the Registrar-General of births, marriages, and deaths, and under the same law he and his deputies were first authorised to license and supervise civil marriages.[19] As Clerk and

---

18.   Havet, 1878 82–84; Commission 1846, 1848 297.

19.   Presently operating under the *Loi ayant rapport aux marriages célébrés dans les Iles de Guernesey, d'Aurigny et de Serk*, 1919, as regulated by the *Loi sur les empêchements au mariage à cause de parenté et sur l'etablissement de la juridiction civile dans les causes matrimoniales*, 1936, and associated laws and amendments.

Registrar of the States, the Greffier distributes *Billets d'État*, records and publishes States' resolutions and orders, and administers ballots.

Her Majesty's Sheriff (the *Prévôt*)

The States no longer elect H.M. Sheriff, or *Prévôt*, as they anciently did. *The Appointment of Her Majesty's Sheriff (Guernsey) Law*, 1955 transferred the power of appointment to the States Appointment Board. It was later entrusted to the Civil Service Board, under the *Appointments Board (Repeal) (Guernsey) Law*, 2000, and is now the responsibility of the Policy Council, under *The Machinery of Government (Transfer of Functions) (Guernsey) Ordinance*, 2003. It remains the case that the holder may only be dismissed by the sovereign's command. The Sheriff is responsible for keeping order in the States of Deliberation and Election, and, as stated in the 1948 Reform Law, is under the direction of 'the President of either assembly in the fulfilment of any ministerial functions required to be exercised by them for or on behalf of either assembly'. The Sheriff receives and announces Royalty and the Lieutenant-Governor when they attend meetings of the States or Court, and declares Royal Proclamations. The Sheriff attends all Royal Court sittings in person or, more often, by deputy, and brings to Court people who have failed to answer summonses. It is the Sheriff's duty to put sentences into effect, and to collect fines. In executing judgments the Sheriff will as necessary arrest goods and sell the same. The Sheriff also represents defaulters and creditors in certain insolvency proceedings. The office in its judicial aspects is comparable to that of the *Sergent de l'Epée* of the ancient courts of Normandy.[20]

Her Majesty's Sergeant

The Lieutenant-Governor appoints the Sergeant, by warrant. The office is not mentioned in ancient sources, although both Laurent Carey and Julien Havet sought to identify it with the king's *bedel*, mentioned in the

---

20. See the Royal Court judgment of 22 December 1977 in the matter of *Chambers v Her Majesty's Sheriff*, and the authorities there cited.

Précepte.[21] It is clear, however, that by the later sixteenth century the Sergeant's duties were well established.[22] H.M. Sergeant is an officer of the States and the Courts, having duties similar to those of the Sheriff, to whom the Sergeant is habitually sworn in as deputy, and there is no bar on both offices being concurrently held by the same person, as is presently the case. The particular responsibilities of the office of Sergeant include attending court sessions, keeping order, serving summonses and other legal notices,[23] and acting as judicial attorney for absent debtors.

The Advocates

The legal profession in Guernsey is fused, which is to say that Advocates of the Guernsey Bar undertake work carried out in some jurisdictions by both barristers and solicitors. They plead in civil and criminal causes, having the exclusive right of appearance before the courts of the Bailiwick of Guernsey.[24] A body of Advocates of the Royal Court is recorded as early as 1323.[25] From the eighteenth century, and perhaps before, until the end of the nineteenth century their number was limited to six.[26] Now there are more than one hundred. Before admission in Guernsey, an Advocate is required to be a member of one of the English and Welsh, Northern Irish, or Scottish, Bars, or to have been admitted as a solicitor in one of those jurisdictions. He or she has to obtain the

---

21. Carey, 1889 46; Havet, 1878 100. The Sergeant's should not be understood as an office analogous to that of the English beadle of more modern times, rather as having functions matching those of the Norman *huissier*; on which see Hoüard, 1780–82 II 715–18.

22. Tramalier, 1715 10–11; Devyck, 1583 5r–5v.

23. Before the coming into force of an Order in Council of 6 October 1849 H.M. Sergeant served summonses only on Crown fiefs, with the sergeants of privately owned fiefs being responsible for the same duty there.

24. Note however that (i) Section 19 of *The Legal Aid (Bailiwick of Guernsey) Law*, 2003, provides that the States may by Ordinance, with the approval of the Royal Court, appoint an 'authorised lawyer' to act for legally assisted persons, and (ii) the Judicial Committee of the Privy Council will hear non-Guernsey counsel in Bailiwick causes.

25. Havet, 1878 79.

26. Cf. de Cléry, 1898 261–73. An Ordinance of 6 October 1777 limited the number to six, but the rule may have been observed as early as 1629, when there were that number in practice, Heylyn prettily observing that the Guernsey people ' . . . conceiving rightly, that multitudes of lawyers make multitudes of business; or according to that merry saying of old Haywood, "the more spaniels in the field, the more game"': Heylyn, 1656 309.

Certificat d'études juridiques françaises et normandes of the Université de Caen, or hold a *Licence* or *Maîtrise en Droit* of one of the Universities of France, and successfully complete the Guernsey Bar Examinations. Residency and pupillage requirements also exist.

The Advocates are regulated by *The Bar Ordinances*, 1932 and 1949, as amended. Their oath obliges them to offer counsel without fear or favour, although only in cases that they regard as good and lawful, and they are to abandon any cause that they should learn to be bad. They are not to declare facts that those instructing them have not avowed to be true, nor should they advise or plead things they do not believe to be so. They are obliged to make known to the Royal Court matters that may affect the Crown. They should not make bargains with clients for a share of amounts awarded, nor involve themselves in judgments in cases upon which they have formerly advised, presumably should one become a judge or Jurat, although they should give their honest and unbiased opinion on anything the Court asks. Unlike the Jurats, advocates have no right to continued enjoyment of the privileges and honours of office once removed from the roll of practitioners, whether upon retirement or for some other reason.

Members of the Guernsey Bar have met formally and kept records of meetings since 5 October 1904. By resolution of 25 June 1993, they constituted the Bar Council as a professional representative body, under the leadership of one of the more senior of them, serving as *Bâtonnier*. The Council, by virtue of *The Royal Court (Bar Administration) Order*, 1993, has powers to make regulations binding on members, subject to the endorsement of the Bailiff and a Law Officer of the Crown. These include Rules of Professional Conduct that have been effective since 1995. In matters of discipline the Advocates are subject to an *ad hoc* disciplinary committee (the *Chambre de Discipline*) normally composed of a Law Officer and two members of the Bar, operating under the *Ordonnance relative au Barreau et au Corps des Ecrivains*, 1932, as amended.[27] The *Chambre* will refer serious cases to the Royal Court for determination. The opinion has been expressed that this regulation of the

---

27. In 1867 the Royal Court established a *corps des écrivains* allowing individuals to be licensed to prepare certain legal documents. This provision was abolished by an Ordinance of 1914, made permanent as the *Ordonnance relative au Barreau et au Corps des Ecrivains*, 1932. This permitted existing practitioners to continue working, and the work of *écrivains* came before the Court as late as the nineteen-seventies.

profession by the profession is incompatible with modern standards, and it is anticipated that the *Chambre de Discipline* will be replaced, or radically remodelled – and perhaps renamed – quite soon.

7. The Law of Guernsey

The sources of Guernsey law are legislative, contained in Royal
Charters, Orders in Council, Acts of Parliament extending to the island,
Ordinances, and Statutory Instruments made under such legislation,[1]
and customary, drawn both from Normandy, and from local laws,
liberties, and usages.

The Customary law

Customary law (*coutume*) has been defined as being of oral legal usage,
time-hallowed, and accepted by the population of a defined territory.[2] In
the course of time some such French *coutumes* were collected together, in
writing, and several of these were endorsed formally by codification and
legislative enactment, and/or embodied in private compilations, these
latter being known as *coutumiers*. Although originating in unwritten
tradition, a *coutume* might also recognise and allow for the creation and
development of law by written enactment and varying usage.

The first known reference to Guernsey's Royal Court is in a charter of
1179 confirming a gift of land to the Abbey of Mont St Michel, made
before the lord the king's Court in Guernsey (*in curia domini Regis in
Guenerreio*) sealed by the island's *Vicomte* and witnessed by other
notables.[3] Before the separation from Normandy, a single such *Vicomte*
appears to have administered the Channel Islands, operating the Courts
in concert with itinerant justices visiting periodically from Normandy.[4]
Triennial assizes continued to be held in the thirteenth century, although

---

1. International treaties and conventions, which are introduced into island law by
locally registered enactments falling within some of these categories, are treated in
Chapter 11, below.
2. Timbal and Castaldo, 1990 330; cf. Sabine, 1948 181–84, and for a
comprehensive treatment de Ferrière, 1762, 412–19.
3. De Guérin, 1919. The charter survives in the archives of Exeter Cathedral,
under reference D&C 2063.
4. Le Patourel, 1937 27–28.

under local officers. From 1299, however, less regular general eyres (ambulatory commissions directed by the king to hear all general causes) often employing non-local justices, took assizes and other pleas, including, novelly, those of *quo warranto*.[5] This questioning of their rights was perceived by the islanders to be contrary to Guernsey's constitution, and forcefully resisted.

A profound study of Channel Islanders' statements to the compilers of inquisitions, surveys of Crown properties and rights and revenues (*extentes*), and the records of general eyres, allowed Professor John Le Patourel, FBA, (1909–81), to describe Guernsey's Medieval constitution with authority. He revealed its essence to be in the islanders' right to have the Jurats participate in all judgments of the king's courts in the island, the people's exemption from answering summonses to secular courts anywhere else, and, in consideration of a payment called *farm*, freedom from certain pecuniary impositions, and military service, unless to accompany the sovereign in person to recover England, or that the sovereign be a captive.[6] Whilst there were necessary innovations in John's reign, these merely modified older customs, which had, in all likelihood, themselves been reorganised at the time of Geoffrey Plantagenet's mid twelfth-century occupation of Normandy, including its islands. Le Patourel suggested that the rights of the islanders originated a century earlier, when the Duke of Normandy may have offered favourable terms to people willing to settle the Channel Islands after depopulation in the Viking era.[7] In short, 'all the Islanders' liberties may be resolved into the general principle that they should be judged by their own law'.[8] In 1299, 1309, and 1331 (the date of the last general eyre) the king and his justices called upon the people of Guernsey to define this law.[9] Whilst the information was not supplied, it is abundantly clear from evidence that in this period the law of Guernsey was that of Normandy, with certain local usages and customs in effect, as was the

---

5. Le Patourel, 1937 42, 54; Crook, 1982 191–93.
6. Le Patourel, 1937 78, 106–10.
7. Le Patourel, 1937 109.
8. Le Patourel, 1937 110; cf. Le Patourel, 1946 7, Le Patourel, 1962 204–08. For a robust eighteenth-century view of Guernsey's rights on the basis that the island is not a conquered territory of the English king, but rather the opposite, see Carey, 1889 2–3.
9. De Guérin, 1909 ii 100–09.

case in the other districts of the province.[10] The substantive law of both the Norman mainland and its islands was described in the *Grand Coutumier de Normandie*, a compilation brought together at a date between 1235 and 1258.[11]

The Bailiwick Seal

Although, apparently since the reign of John, it had been possible to initiate most suits in the Royal Court without need of the king's writ,[12] under cover of a charter dated 15 November 1279, Edward I found it desirable to send a seal of his own to the Channel Islands for the use of their respective courts, so

> ... that in future the writs which the men of the Islands aforesaid hitherto were wont to obtain in Our Chancery of England, and which from henceforth they may wish to obtain, and the agreements and contracts which from now shall happen to be made from time to time there, and which hitherto were wont to be made verbally, and not by writing, from henceforth shall be sealed with the same seal. ... And therefore we command you that you receive that seal, and that you cause to be publicly proclaimed throughout all the land of the Islands aforesaid that those of those parts who from henceforth shall wish to have Our writs aforesaid shall obtain them there according to the ancient register of the same parts, as hitherto they have been wont to do in Our Chancery aforesaid. And you the Bailiffs aforesaid from this time shall cause such writs, agreements, and contracts to be sealed with the same seal ...[13]

Circa 1304, the separate Bailiwicks, probably for reasons of convenience, started using a seal each.[14] Though a few writs continued to be issued out of Chancery – and the Bailiwick Seal not standing for the Great Seal, it

---

10. Le Patourel, 1941; 1962.
11. Musset, 1982 6. Strictly speaking, it is the Latin *Summa de Legibus Normannie in Curia Laicali* (Tardif, 1896) as it has come to be known, that is datable to the period 1235–58, the *Grand Coutumier* being the *Summa*'s French translation, which is datable to the period 1270–1302. This French version is most accessible in the edition of de Gruchy, 1881.
12. This is explained with admirable clarity in Holt and Everard, 2004 160–62.
13. Translated from the Latin, Curtis, 1939 256.
14. Le Patourel, 1937 52.

could hardly be otherwise[15] – it remains the case today that agreements, contracts, orders and judgments properly published by the Royal Court are attested under a representation of the seal first granted in 1279.[16]

The assertion of rights

On 13 February 1218 the regency council of Henry III gave notice that new assizes were not at that time intended for the Channel Islands, but that the assizes should be observed as in the time of Henry II, Richard, and John. Dr Everard and Professor Holt have recently pointed out that this amounted to an undertaking 'not to introduce new laws or innovations in the exercise of royal jurisdiction, substantive or procedural', at least for the time being,[17] and on 8 May 1221, the Warden of the Islands was commanded by the king to 'rule the Islanders by right and due customs, as they have been accustomed to be ruled in the time of our ancestors, kings of England'.[18] This was no mere form of words, and a century later the Jurats and other Guernsey citizens gaoled a sub-warden sent by the king on the grounds that his letters of appointment did not state that he was to act according to the laws and customs of the island. The Justices Itinerant serving between the reigns of Henry II and Edward III were all directed that their assizes should observe these laws and customs. These then were the circumstances in which the Islanders took such grave exception to the Justices investigating, *quo warranto*, immemorial usages as if they were mere franchises allowed by the king, rather than enjoyed as of right.[19]

After consequent unrest, on 10 July 1341 Edward III, eager to maintain the loyalty of the islanders on engaging upon war with France,[20] published a charter confirming to the Channel Islanders generally

---

15. Cf. Chaplais, 1957 63; Thornton, 2002 205.
16. Cf. Havet, 1878 159–64. Le Patourel, 1937 43 n. 7 makes the point that it is unlikely that original writs were ever issued by the Channel Islands' courts.
17. Everard and Holt, 2004 164.
18. Le Patourel, 1937 36, quoting and translating part of a writ addressed to Philip d'Aubigny the younger. The original is on the English Patent Rolls.
19. Le Patourel, 1937 50–59.
20. De Guérin, 1909 ii 108. Castle Cornet was at this date occupied by the French.

... that they themselves, their heirs and successors may have and hold all privileges, liberties, immunities, exemptions, and customs in respect of their persons, goods, moneys, and other matters by virtue of the grant of our progenitors kings of England or otherwise lawfully by agreement, and, without impediment or molestation from us, our heirs or our officers whomsoever, may fully enjoy and use them according as they themselves and their predecessors, inhabitants of the said islands, have reasonably used and enjoyed them ...[21]

The English Patent Rolls, under date of 14 July 1349, record the unsalaried appointment for life of one Peter Guyon to the duty of bearing the mace (*clavum*) in Guernsey. This, presumably, had a connection with the operation of the Royal Court in the island, although what happened to the office, and equally the mace, remains unknown.

The *Précepte d'Assize*

On 30 September 1441, the Royal Court published the document known as the *Précepte d'Assize*.[22] This purported to be a statement of the usages, customs, and constitution of Guernsey, approved by the Justices of 1331. In this claim, it seems that it was incorrect; there is no earlier mention of such a thing, whether in the records of the Justices or elsewhere, and it might be argued that in the *Précepte* we see the Court asserting its position in a period of particular English care for the Islands, as evidenced by Henry VI's grant on 10 February 1442 of a charter that revived fourteenth-century customs privileges, and in 1443 the confirmation that Islanders were no longer to be taxed in England as the aliens that they had been deemed to be in 1440.[23] Whatever the context of its content, the *Précepte* nonetheless has the appearance of an accurate statement of long-standing procedures and conventions, and it has repeatedly been endorsed as such. Certainly, by the end of the fourteenth century the power of the Royal Court of Guernsey was well defined. Le Patourel concluded that by that time although it exercised powers

---

21. Thornton, 2004 3–4, translated from the Latin.
22. De Havilland, 1847; de Sausmarez, 1934 130–50. The original is lost. There is a formally collated copy dated 25 September 1489 in Guernsey's Greffe.
23. Thornton, 2004 20–21, where Henry VI's likely motives in favouring the islands are also treated.

formally granted to the Warden, the Court was largely independent in its jurisdiction in all pleas.[24]

The *Approbation des Loix*

Economic and commercial problems in Guernsey in the later 1570s appear to have led to quite a degree of unrest, so much so that in 1578, or perhaps early in the next year, the Bailiff and Jurats requested the Privy Council to issue an order requiring the Royal Court to follow the island's inherited law, to reform abuses, and secure the obedience of the people. At about the same time some islanders appeared before the Council, seeking to remedy certain private grievances, and a similar reform of the administration of justice.[25] A Royal Commission was appointed on 27 July 1579 to deal with these and other issues, and to seek clarification, in a manner reminiscent of the demands of the thirteenth and fourteenth centuries, of the extent to which the customs and laws of Normandy applied in the island, save as was otherwise provided in *extentes* and the *Précepte*. The Commission's report, sent from Guernsey to the Lord Chancellor on 9 October 1579, annexes statements, which, though unattributed, were clearly the work of the Royal Court, or at least some of its members.[26] These refer at length to the thirteenth-century *Grand Coutumier de Normandie*. For reasons that perhaps related to the antiquity and redundancy of aspects of the *Grand Coutumier*, the statements were not accepted by the Privy Council, and on 9 October 1580 it ordered that the Court should direct itself according to the *Précepte* and the *extente* of 1331, in so far as these were not repugnant to Royal or Council orders. With regard to the many matters not addressed by the *Précepte* and *extente*, in these the Court was enjoined for the time being to follow the *Grand Coutumier*. A necessary exception for differing local practice was allowed, however, and it was ordered that Guernsey's particular laws and customs should again be set out in writing and sent to the Privy Council. A further order, of 30 July 1581, assigned this task to the Bailiff and Jurats, the Governor or his

---

24. Le Patourel, 1937 67.
25. Eagleston, 1949 74–81.
26. Commission 1579, 1579 12r-28v. For the attribution, see the comments of the Commissioner Dr John Hammond preserved in British Library, Department of Manuscripts, Lansdowne MS 657.

lieutenant, and Her Majesty's Procureur.[27] The Royal Court – by now under a new Bailiff – and the Governor prepared a further document, on this occasion consulting the most up-to-date commentary on the law of Normandy, namely Guillaume Terrien's *Commentaires du Droict Civil tant public que privé, observé au pays et Duché de Normandie*, which had been published in Paris in 1574.[28] Terrien (d. 1573 or '74) had been *lieutenant-général du bailli de Dieppe*, and in the book he treated the *Grand Coutumier*, and also the fifteenth-century *Style de Procéder*, the *Style de Parlement* (1515) and numerous ordinances of the kings of France.[29] The Guernsey authorities took Terrien's work chapter by chapter (as they had a few years earlier taken the *Grand Coutumier* chapter by chapter) and commented to a greater or lesser degree on his text and its application to, and variance from, the laws, customs, and usages of Guernsey. The result was submitted to the Privy Council, which on 27 October 1583 'ratified and approved ... the laws and customs therein contained', saving

> ... always to Her Majesty and to her heirs and successors power to add, diminish and correct them at her good pleasure, reserving likewise all other privileges, profits, rights and prerogatives belonging to Her said Majesty, her heirs and successors, nevertheless without causing any prejudice to the ancient and legitimate privileges heretofore granted to the inhabitants of the said island ...[30]

The commentary on Terrien's *Commentaires* and this approval by the Privy Council together form that statement of Guernsey law known as the *Approbation des Loix*. (H.M. Procureur at the time, Louis Devyck, did not sign the copy of the submission to the Privy Council now in the Greffe. He wrote a third statement of the law of Guernsey, including a lengthy commentary on the *Grand Coutumier*, which although in this

---

27.   Commission 1846, 1848 313–16.
28.   Reprinted, with the same pagination, at Paris, 1578, and Rouen, 1654.
29.   Le Verdier, n.d.; Besnier, 1935 153–54.
30.   Tramalier, 1715 43, translated from the French. The approbation was given notwithstanding the objections to the use of Terrien's work raised in the opinion and report presented to the Council by the Royal Commission's legal member, Dr John Hammond (1542–89), which survives in the British Library Department of Manuscripts in Lansdowne MS 657 and cf. Commission 1846, 1848 viii–x.

case also 'approuvé' by the Privy Council, on 30 October 1583, did not and does not bear the authority of the *Approbation des Loix*).[31]

The modern law

The modern law of Guernsey is founded upon the thirteenth-century *Grand Coutumier de Normandie* and other laws, customs, and usages, as presented by Guillaume Terrien and in the *Approbation des Loix*. These customs and usages include those recognised by Royal Charter and/or convention, such as some set out in the *extente* of Royal Revenues of 1331 and the *Précepte* of 1441, to both of which constitutional documents the *Approbation* refers. This is not by any means to say that the law of the island is set in a sixteenth-century aspic. Customary law systems such as Guernsey's are susceptible to alteration through time, and may be modified not only by written enactments, but also by varying usage and non-usage (ie. *custom* in one of its definitions) including judicial decision and the influence of evolving law elsewhere.[32]

Although not bound by the doctrine of *stare decisis* to the extent of their English counterparts, the Bailiwick's courts do have regard to local precedents, and the decisions of superior Guernsey courts bind lower ones. Precedents and comparisons drawn from the laws and practices of other jurisdictions, especially those of Jersey, England and Wales, Scotland, and other Commonwealth countries, are also often cited by advocates, and considered to be of persuasive value, though not uncritically, by the courts. The influence of the English Common Law has been most marked historically in criminal matters,[33] although today English precedents and legal concepts inform civil pleadings and judgments in other areas as well. Trust law and the law of torts, for example, have developed in largely English form (although it was necessary to codify the law of trusts in 1989).[34] In other areas,

---

31. Devyck, 1583.
32. Routier, 1748 3; cf. Nicolle, 1999 sect. 12; Morgan, 1997. This last notices the landmark Guernsey Court of Appeal judgment in the matter of *Morton v Paint*, delivered 9 February 1996. Entire written and other constitutions are themselves susceptible to similar alteration: 'Constitutions may be supplemented or modified or even nullified by usages, customs, and conventions' (Wheare, 1966 4).
33. Gahan, 1963.
34. By *The Trusts (Guernsey) Law*, 1989. See also the policy letter of the States Advisory and Finance Committee published in *Billet d'État* ix 1988 (17 March) 244–

particularly land law and the law of inheritance, the Norman element is resilient.[35] The influence of English law may be accounted for by several particular factors, including the fact that advocates are trained as English barristers or solicitors, the Guernsey Court of Appeal includes senior English counsel amongst its judges, and that reports of English cases, which are often cited, are more sophisticated and profuse than Guernsey ones, and are readily accessible.

Legislation

As stated above, the enacted law is contained in Royal Charters, Orders in Council, Acts of Parliament extending to Guernsey, Ordinances, and Statutory Instruments made under such legislation.

Royal Charters

Edward III's charter of 1341 was repeated, confirmed, and extended, particularly with regard to Islanders' exemptions from English tolls, by succeeding sovereigns up to and including Elizabeth I, who published a charter for Guernsey, dated 29 July 1559, confirming certain earlier ones.[36] On 15 March 1560, she issued, by the authority of Parliament, a fuller confirmation of the *status quo*.[37] Noting that the Bailiwick of Guernsey had

> ... from time beyond what the memory of men can reach, by virtue of several charters, grants, confirmations, and most ample writs, of our illustrious progenitors and ancestors, both kings of England and dukes of Normandy, and others, have used, enjoyed, and been in possession of very many rights, jurisdictions, privileges, immunities, liberties, and

---

46. In 1860, Advocate Peter Jeremie indicated that trusts in the English sense were a recent innovation in Guernsey, and noted a need for their regulation: Jeremie, 1861 679.

35. With regard to inheritance, see, for example, Ashley, 1953 273–93, and Poirey, 1997. Unfortunately Guernsey's land law has not been the subject of similar academic interest.

36. Thornton, 2004 78–83.

37. Thornton, 2004 77–78 plausibly suggests that this second charter was obtained at the suit of members of the island's Protestant party, who did not come to secular power until 1565. Ogier, 1996 signally failed to notice the likelihood of this.

franchises, freely, quietly, and without any infringement of the same
. . .[38]

the Queen confirmed at length, subject to existing Royal interests, the
Bailiwick's right to its own courts, with local cases being heard locally
and natives immune from summons to foreign courts in causes arising in
the islands, the inhabitants' exemption from English taxation, and
ordinary military service abroad, and the privilege of trading with all
sides in times of war, this last having arisen in consequence of a Papal
Bull of 1481, as referred to in the introduction to this work.

The charter of 1560, made by the authority of Parliament, stated the
Queen granted it for herself and her successors, and its terms were
confirmed in a series of charters, ending with that of Charles II of 11
February 1668.[39] They were significantly modified only by an Order in
Council of 8 August 1689, which confirmed that a recent prohibition on
importing goods from France should be observed in the Channel Islands,
hence contradicting, or at least suspending, the privilege of neutrality.
This appears to have been acceptable to the islanders, who were assured
'it is not the intention of his majesty in any manner whatsoever to revoke
or infringe upon any privileges that may have been granted by his royal
predecessors to the inhabitants of the said island of Guernsey'.[40] A
vigorous privateering enterprise promptly developed.[41] The relatively
recent privilege of neutrality being the only part of the charters to be
actively revoked, it might be inferred that a provision of the Bill of
Rights (1689) that charters, grants, and pardons issued before 23
October 1689 should remain in force and effect in law, acted to confirm
from Parliament's point of view the Bailiwick's constitutional *status quo*.

Other enactments have also confirmed aspects of Guernsey's
constitution. On 22 June 1565, the Privy Council, having received
complaints that the Channel Islands' 'ancient charters and liberties'
(confirmed for Guernsey only five years before) were being breached by
judgments awarded contrary to them in English Courts, and that appeals
were coming before such courts, ordered, after receiving the opinion of
the Solicitor-General and the Lords Chief Justice:

---

38. Thornton, 2004 89, translated from the Latin.
39. Thornton, 2004 144–70.
40. Duncan, 1841 229–30.
41. Bromley, 1986.

... that from henceforth all suits commenced there already or hereafter to be commenced between any subjects of these isles, should be heard, ordered and adjudged in the same isles, and not within this realm, and the like order their lordships determined should be kept in suits arising and concerning two parties, whereof one is resident here in England and the other in the said isles, and further their lordships resolved that no appeals should be made from any sentence in judgment given in the same isles hither, but only according to the words of their charters, *au Roi et son Conseil*, which agrees, as Sir Hugh Powlet [the Governor of Jersey] alleges, with such order and form as has heretofore been accustomed ...[42]

These terms were reiterated, although by reference to the Royal Charter of 1560, in the preamble to *The Judgments (Reciprocal Enforcement) (Guernsey) Law*, 1957.

The Channel Islands' chartered customs immunities in English ports were also confirmed, for the avoidance of doubt, under section five of the Act of Parliament concerning duties, 3 George I c. 4, 1716. At this Act's repeal, specific provisions were made for the continuance of established usages, and they were again confirmed under the Act to Consolidate the Customs Laws 1876, and the Customs and Excise Duties (General Reliefs) Act 1979. Similarly, the immunity of Islanders from military service abroad, unless to accompany the sovereign in person to recover England, or the sovereign be a captive, was confirmed by an Order in Council of 6 November 1916, and reiterated in the preamble to *The National Service (Guernsey) Law*, 1954.

Orders in Council

Orders in Council may be classified under the following headings:

(a) Judicial Orders, giving effect to judgments of the Judicial Committee of the Privy Council,

(b) Administrative Orders, settling administrative disputes,

(c) Legislative Orders, requiring things to be done,

---

42. Dasent, 1893 224. As already noted, the word 'alleges' in this passage is used in the sense of a declaration of the law.

(d) Extending or applying orders, extending Acts of Parliament, statutory instruments, church measures, international conventions, treaties, etc. to the island, and

(e) Sanctioning Orders, sanctioning insular legislation.[43]

Class (a) is referred to in Chapter five, above. Administrative Orders concern relatively early directions of the Privy Council, for example some of the Orders made in 1608 attendant upon the recommendations of the Royal Commission appointed in the previous year, as mentioned in Chapter nine. Legislative Orders were made increasingly rarely after the mid nineteenth century, when their propriety became an issue. The last such was the Court of Appeal (Channel Islands) Order 1949, made on the recommendation of the Committee of the Privy Council that visited the Islands in 1946, which brought in a scheme that had been approved by States' meetings in both Guernsey and Jersey. As noted in Chapter five, the Order was later revoked, and it would appear that today the power of the Privy Council to make such Orders is limited, perhaps almost extinguished, by convention, and constitutional and democratic principles. Extending Orders are discussed in Chapter nine. Class (e), referring to the process of how Orders in Council give effect to *Projets de Loi*, has been described in Chapter four.

Acts of Parliament extending to Guernsey

Historically, the United Kingdom Parliament legislated for the Channel Islands only by Acts that specifically named them, or which by necessary implication applied to them (for example Succession Acts). Mr Hocart notes a particular tendency to regulate the island's trade by Act of Parliament in the early nineteenth century.[44] It was usual at that time for the Clerk of the Privy Council to convey Acts of Parliament to Guernsey's Royal Court for registration. As will be seen in Chapter nine, below, it was a controversial question whether registration was necessary for an Act to take effect in law. Here it will suffice to say that more commonly, particularly in the twentieth century, Acts were not transmitted simply under cover of an Order, but were drafted with a

---

43. I have here adopted and adapted Dr Heyting's scheme for Jersey (Heyting, 1977 83).
44. Hocart, 1988 20.

section allowing for extension to the Channel Islands by Order in Council. This allowed the Islands to make representations, should it have been thought inappropriate that any particular Act should be extended. It also allowed at the drafting stage consideration of any modifications that may have been required to meet the Islands' needs, administrative systems, and legal procedures. In cases where Acts gave powers to Ministers, Secretaries of State, or the Privy Council to make subordinate statutory instruments, it was usual for the Order in Council extending the legislation to provide that such measures should not be effective until registration by the Royal Court.[45] Recently, hardly any Acts of Parliament have been extended directly to the Channel Islands, and very few by Order in Council. Rather, the local legislatures promote their own laws mirroring Acts as appropriate.[46] Examples include laws relating to human rights, the proceeds of crime, data protection, and terrorism.

Ordinances

The process by which Ordinances are made was described in Chapter four. The States, as successors in this function after 1948 to the Royal Court, do this under the authority of customary law, or by enabling powers under Orders in Council. Orders in Council themselves are often brought into force on a day appointed by the States by Ordinance. Ordinances may be original legislation,[47] and, as confirmed by an Order in Council of 1936, may set punitive sentences, including terms of imprisonment (as was commonly the case in the Early Modern period).[48] Increasingly, Orders in Council contain enabling provisions allowing their modification by way of Ordinance, and under the *The Human Rights (Implementation and Amendment) (Bailiwick of Guernsey) Law,* 2004, which itself is due to be brought into force by Ordinance, the States will in future be able by Ordinance to modify non-human rights compliant sections of Orders in Council. European Community regulations are also implemented by Ordinance. Modern Ordinances

---

45. Loveridge, 174 395–96.
46. Edwards, 1998 iii 3; Lord Chancellor's Department, 2002 paras 36–38.
47. Loveridge, 1974 397.
48. Ogier, 1996 ch.6.

sometimes can, therefore, in the same manner as other legislation and practices, modify the customary law.

Statutory Instruments

A variety of secondary legislation is created under statutory authority. This is to say that certain Orders in Council, Acts, and Ordinances allow designated persons and bodies to set down further legal requirements and directives, orders, rules, and regulations, generically known as 'Statutory Instruments'. Those created under United Kingdom Acts of Parliament are rarely made: an example would be an air navigation order made under the Civil Aviation Act 1982. These are transmitted to the Royal Court and registered at the Greffe. More common are orders etc. made by statutory authorities in Guernsey, ranging from regulations relating to rubbish collection, to instruments governing data protection. These are laid before the States by the Policy Council and Departments, and lodged at the Greffe, under the terms of *The Guernsey Statutory Instruments (Registration) Ordinance*, 1949.

The modern law of Guernsey

Any discussion of Guernsey's government is inseparable from the discussion of its law. As has been stated, the essence of Guernsey's ancient polity was that 'all the Islanders' liberties may be resolved into the general principle that they should be judged by their own law'.[49] This remains the case today. The island's own law was and is mutable, and there are now incorporated into it, in varying degrees, international, European, and United Kingdom elements. These elements, assimilating with the Norman law and longstanding local usages, enmesh to make the modern, still developing, law of Guernsey.

---

49.   Le Patourel, 1937 110.

8. Guernsey and the Channel Islands

Inter-Bailiwick relations

The nature of Guernsey's relations with its nearest neighbours varies from island to island. Formal relations with Jersey are few. The islands were not jointly under the administration of a single English Warden appointed after 1473.[1] By this date, their Royal Courts had evolved separately for a considerable time. The States' assemblies in each island similarly appear to have developed independently of each other.

There is an agreement between the respective Bailiwicks concerning the median line between them, and complementary Guernsey and Jersey legislation provides for the holding of Channel Islands' lotteries. An annual meeting is held between members of Guernsey's Policy Council, accompanied by the Chief Executive of the States of Guernsey, and often one of the Law Officers of the Crown, and the equivalent functionaries in the other Crown Dependencies, at which tax and economic subjects, and aspects of relations with the United Kingdom and various international bodies are discussed. The Bailiffs of the islands will confer routinely on judicial developments in their respective jurisdictions that may be of common interest, and will discuss the names of persons put forward as possible judges of the separate Courts of Appeal. Exceptionally they will meet on issues with constitutional implications common to both jurisdictions, and each usually serves as a judge of the Court of Appeal in the other's island. The Deputy Bailiffs and Law Officers of the Crown in both Bailiwicks similarly meet to discuss matters such as concern the judiciary and constitutional affairs. The United Kingdom's Lord Chancellor's Department has met with officials of all of the Crown Dependencies periodically, and doubtless the Department for Constitutional Affairs which has succeeded the Lord Chancellor's Department will continue to do so. When a need is perceived to present a united front internationally, the Channel Islands' authorities will also work together.

---

1. Thornton, 2004 46.

This has been particularly noticeable in recent years, where close consultation has accompanied Channel Islands' negotiations with bodies such as the European Union, the Organisation for Economic Co-operation and Development, and the Financial Action Task Force.

Relations within the Bailiwick

Not surprisingly, Guernsey's formal relations with the other principal islands of its Bailiwick, namely Alderney and Sark, are closer than they are with the distinct Bailiwick of Jersey.

Guernsey and Alderney[2]

In the fourteenth century, the Court of Alderney was administered by a Prévôt, appointed by the Warden. It had seven Jurats. When called upon to judge crimes of serious violence, the Court's Jurats sat with the Bailiff of Guernsey. The Alderney Jurats were also obliged to consult their counterparts in Guernsey when they were doubtful about any point of law.[3] By the later sixteenth century, the office of Prévôt in Alderney is said to have disappeared, and judgments were apparently made by six, or seven, jurats. The Court's relationship with the Royal Court of Guernsey also appears to have changed, as suggested by the orders of Commissioners appointed in 1585 by the Privy Council. These required the Alderney Jurats to administer justice in all causes arising in the island according to the law and constitution of Guernsey, lately codified by the *Approbation des Loix*, at the same time allowing appeals to be made to the Royal Court, and referring criminal causes to it.[4]

The report of the Royal Commission of 1846 revealed that at that date the relationship between the Alderney Court and Guernsey's Royal Court remained much the same as in the later sixteenth century. The Alderney Court had a full civil jurisdiction, subject to a right of appeal to Guernsey. In any criminal cause, the Court was merely able to determine whether there was a *prima facie* case to answer, and if so refer it to the Royal Court. It was then necessary to take the accused to Guernsey, and for the Royal Court to inspect depositions. If a trial ensued, witnesses

2. See now van Leuven, 2004.
3. Le Patourel, 1937 101–02.
4. MacCulloch and Métivier, 1938 10.

were conveyed to Guernsey.[5] In 1848 and 1850, Orders in Council rationalised affairs, granting to the Alderney Court a limited criminal jurisdiction, similar to that then exercised by Guernsey's Royal Court sitting as an Ordinary Court.

Alderney's States and Court also traditionally enjoyed a limited power to make Ordinances. Examples survive from the eighteenth century, and perhaps others were made in earlier times.[6] In 1821, Guernsey's Royal Court confirmed this power, although at the same time the latter did have the right to modify or annul Alderney Ordinances. The smaller jurisdiction's authorities are also known, on at least one occasion in the nineteenth century, to have petitioned the Privy Council, successfully submitting a *Projet de Loi* for the making of an Order in Council applicable to their island.[7]

By the early twentieth century, all draft laws, save those relating to finance, were submitted by Alderney to Guernsey's Royal Court for approval. In the pressing conditions of the Great War, however, the practice developed that *Projets* were submitted directly to the Lieutenant-Governor for transmission to the Home Office and eventual Privy Council approval. By the nineteen-twenties, according to a memorandum prepared by the Lieutenant-Governor, conveyed to Guernsey's Bailiff with a letter dated 21 February 1924, it was then the case that the States of Alderney regularly made criminal laws and Ordinances, and even modified their island's constitution, without reference to the Royal Court.[8] After submission to the Privy Council, some of these *Projets* had been embodied in Orders in Council. The capacity of the States of Alderney in such matters was far from clear, and on 11 March 1925, a meeting was held between representatives of Alderney's administration and Guernsey's Royal Court, on the subject of the respective powers of the two courts. An Order in Council registered in Guernsey on 13 February 1926 sanctioned the agreement then reached. This confirmed the Alderney Court's powers to make Ordinances within certain limits, and those of the Royal Court to set aside any of them it might find to be *ultra vires*. The power of the Alderney States to raise domestic taxes was recognised to be outside the

---

5. Venne and Allez, 1992 94.
6. Commission 1846, 1848 194; MacCulloch and Métivier, 1938 17, 32–33.
7. Commission 1846, 1848 184.
8. Island Archives Service: file BF 6–10.

Royal Court's purview. That the criminal law of Alderney was that of Guernsey, and that Alderney might legislate in relation to it as far as permissible by Ordinance was also confirmed. Civil and constitutional legislation that was the subject of Alderney *Projets de Loi* should be submitted to the Royal Court for comment before transmission to the Privy Council. In instances where a single law, with Alderney's agreement, should apply to both islands, the Bailiff would submit the *Projet* to the Privy Council through the usual channels.

Alderney was seriously dilapidated at the end of the Second World War. The extent of properties could no longer be defined, and neither agriculture nor necessary services were easily to be re-established. An Order of 3 July 1947 created a Committee of the Privy Council to enquire into the situation. Certain solutions proposed by the States of Alderney were not regarded by the Committee as likely to prevent the total dereliction that threatened.[9] At the Committee's request, the Home Secretary visited Alderney in January 1948. Following his informal discussions with the island's authorities, a special committee of the States approached the States of Guernsey to explore the possibility of the larger island taking on responsibility for major services. A similar Guernsey committee endorsed the idea, and both States approved the proposal in principle. A joint committee was established, and following its final meeting, which representatives of the Home Office also attended, enabling legislation was drawn up. The States of Guernsey thus came to assume, under *The Alderney (Application of Legislation) Law,* 1948, financial, legislative, and administrative responsibility for Alderney's airport, health, social and education services, police and immigration, main roads and drains, and water supply, defined in the Law as the 'transferred services'. In 1955, Alderney's States took back responsibility for the main roads, drains, and water supply. Contrastingly, adoption and child care were added to the transferred services in 1974 and 1997 respectively. Guernsey Income Tax and certain indirect taxes, fees, and duties are levied in Alderney, and paid to the States of Guernsey authorities. Guernsey does, however, fund any deficit in Alderney's finances.

---

9. Privy Council, 1949; cf. Packe and Dreyfus, 1971 138–39, and Rowland, 2000 121–25.

The post-war constitutions of Alderney's Court and States were largely the creation of *The Alderney (Application of Legislation) Law*, 1948, and *The Government of Alderney Law*, 1948. A *Billet d'État* of the States of Alderney of 7 May 1986 noted that these measures had been made somewhat hastily. It was proposed that a new law of consolidating, clarifying, and modernising effect should be introduced, and *The Government of Alderney Law*, 1987 was the result. This law, as amended, taken with the 1948 Application of Legislation Law, as also amended, embodies much of the island's modern constitution. The States of Alderney retain powers to create *Projets de Loi* and also Ordinances. These are usually drawn up by the Law Officers of the Crown in Guernsey, although some of the more straightforward Ordinances may be drafted by the Clerk of the States in Alderney, who submits them to the Law Officers for comment and, if necessary, amendment. The States of Guernsey retain and exercise the power to legislate directly in criminal affairs, and in connection with the transferred services. They can also legislate for Alderney in other matters with consent.

The Government of Alderney Law, 1987 also confirmed the Alderney Court's existing jurisdiction in all matters other than the criminal, and in regard to the latter set out the limits within which the Court may try and determine charges, with reference to maximum penalties, whether fines, terms of imprisonment, or both. In matters of treason, homicide, piracy, rape, perjury, or robbery, the Court has no jurisdiction, but is obliged to consider whether there may be a *prima facie* case for the accused to answer. Guernsey's Royal Court sitting as a Full Court hears criminal appeals (the Bailiff sitting alone in appeals from conviction only), and its Ordinary Division adjudicates appeals in other matters.[10]

The Government of Alderney Law, 1987 also provides that in some circumstances, including occasions when a Jurat of the Alderney Court may have a personal interest in a matter under consideration, the Bailiff of Guernsey has the power to appoint a person to exercise the powers of the Court in that matter. Under the same Law, the Bailiff of Guernsey takes precedence over the President of Alderney's States.

---

10. Guernsey's Royal Court also appears to retain the power to declare Ordinances of the Alderney States *ultra vires* (a matter not touched upon in the 1987 Law) following its judgment of 2 December 1977, in *The Law Officers of the Crown v Alderney Meat Products Limited and Drifield Estates Limited*.

The Government of Alderney (Miscellaneous and Consequential Provisions) (Guernsey and Alderney) Law, 1987 repealed the largely otiose agreement between the courts of the two islands of 1925. A Joint Guernsey-Alderney Advisory Council had been created in 1949 to provide consultation and liaison between the States of the two islands. In 1978, the Council lapsed, by agreement. It was revived, as the Joint Guernsey Alderney Consultative Council, to meet as and when necessary, following resolutions of both States of 1995 (amended by the States of Alderney in 1999). Until May 2004, the President of Guernsey's Advisory and Finance Committee, or his delegate, and whomever the States of Alderney appointed, jointly held its presidency. The six other Guernsey delegates represented the Guernsey States' Committees responsible for the transferred services, and the six other Alderney delegates were appointed by that island's States on a meeting-by-meeting basis, having regard to the subjects on the agenda. As part of the wider review of government, a *Billet d'État* placed before a meeting of the States of Guernsey held on 16 May 2003 noted that:

> With regard to the relationship between Guernsey and Alderney, it is anticipated that the Joint Consultative Council would cease to be a standing committee of the States and instead the Policy Council would assume responsibility for liaison on matters relating to the delivery in Alderney of the 'Transferred Services'. It would seek to achieve this by establishing a sub-group comprising the Chief Minister and the Ministers whose departments were responsible for delivering the Alderney transferred services. Alderney would continue to determine which of its representatives met with the Policy Council's sub-group and as at present there would continue to be equality of representation. The joint responsibility of this cross-island group would be to act as a means of consultation and liaison between the States of Guernsey and Alderney. The existing Joint Guernsey and Alderney Consultative Council in its current form would therefore be dissolved.

The Council was duly abolished with effect from 6 May 2004 – from a Guernsey perspective, at least – and a replacement is in the process of formation.

The post-war reforms also provided for the representation of the Alderney States in the States of Guernsey, by *The States of Guernsey (Representation of Alderney) Law*, 1949, now superseded by a like-named law of 1978, as amended. This allows two Alderney Representatives, nominated by the States of Alderney, to sit in Guernsey's States, enjoying the rights and privileges (though not the remuneration) of other members, including the capacity to vote and speak on all matters, including those relating exclusively to Guernsey.

Guernsey and Sark

As in Alderney, a Prévôt, appointed by the Warden, administered the fourteenth-century Court of Sark. There were six Jurats. Whether Sark's Court also had a similar jurisdictional relationship with Guernsey's Royal Court is unknown, though it seems likely that it did.[11] Sark seems to have been depopulated in the later Middle Ages. The island was granted by the Royal Commissioners appointed in May 1563 to Helier de Carteret of Jersey.[12] This award was confirmed by a Royal Charter of 1565, which amongst much else allowed the Seigneur (de Carteret and his successors) the right to a manorial court. This appears to have functioned until 1579, when a short-lived Bailiff's Court, operating according to the usages of Jersey, was set up. An Order in Council of 24 April 1583 imposed a court of five Jurats, with the senior member acting as judge, but this was not brought into effect until 16 July 1594, with the manorial court apparently serving in the meantime. In 1675, the Sénéchal's Court as presently constituted was established.[13]

The Order in Council of 1583 laid down that in administering justice the Sark Jurats should '... apply the laws and customs approved and established by the authority of Her Majesty in the said island of Guernsey, which conforms with the laws and customs of Normandy and with the local customs of the said island of Guernsey, which have been approved, differing from the laws and customs of Normandy'.[14] From this reference to the Order in Council of 9 October 1580, noted in Chapter seven, or perhaps to the *Approbation des Loix* (even though the latter was not to be promulgated formally until some months

---

11. Le Patourel, 1937 101–02.
12. Ogier, 1996 187.
13. Ewen and de Carteret, 1969 49–54, 80; Axton and Axton, 1991 10–11.
14. Ewen and de Carteret, 1969 56, 144–46.

later),[15] the Sark Order moved on to allow the island's Court jurisdiction in minor civil actions. In further resemblance of the Alderney situation, the Order also provided that all criminal causes should be referred to Guernsey's Royal Court.

Guernsey's Royal Court asserted a jurisdiction to regulate procedure in Sark's governing assembly, Chief Pleas, by Ordinance in 1827. In 1832 it acted similarly with regard to appeals from the Sénéchal's Court. However, it was not until the twentieth century that the smaller island's constitution was comprehensively reformed, first by an Order in Council made 20 June 1922, amended by a further Order dated 26 June 1923. The former of these confirmed Chief Pleas' right to make Ordinances, as set out in the Order of 1583, but provided that Guernsey's Royal Court (subject to a right of appeal to the Privy Council) had the power to annul such of them as it might find to be *ultra vires* or unreasonable. The Order also provided for regulation by the Royal Court of Chief Pleas' powers and duties. By an Ordinance of 7 June 1930, made permanent the following year, the Royal Court acknowledged the Sénéchal's Court's full jurisdiction in civil suits, subject to a right of appeal, and conceded to it a criminal jurisdiction in matters attracting only small fines, and such as would not warrant more than three days' imprisonment, or be so grave as to be the Royal Court's responsibility.

The Reform (Sark) Law, 1951, as amended, replaced the 1922 Order, and confirmed the Sénéchal's Court's comprehensive civil jurisdiction, with the right of appeal from its decisions to the Ordinary Division of Guernsey's Royal Court. It also confirmed the Court's competence in criminal matters (subject to a right of appeal to Guernsey's Royal Court sitting as a Full Court) in respect of offences that did not attract a fine of more than a specified sum and/or a certain term of imprisonment. *The Magistrate's Court (Criminal Appeals) (Guernsey) Law*, 1988, now regulates criminal appeals to the Royal Court, requiring that these should be dealt with in the same way as appeals from the Magistrate's Court in Guernsey.

That the Ordinary Division of the Royal Court of Guernsey has an original civil jurisdiction concurrent with that of the Sénéchal's Court is indicated by the latter's referral of the action of *Godfray v the Constables*

---

15.   The return that Guernsey's authorities submitted to the Privy Council is dated 22 May 1582. The Order in Council embodying the *Approbation* was not made until 27 October 1583: Tramalier, 1715 4, 43–44.

of the Island of Sark to the former jurisdiction in 1895.[16] This precedent suggests that the Sénéchal's Court might still, if necessary, transfer certain other cases, for example those of particular complexity, to Guernsey's Royal Court. An alternative recently endorsed in principle by Sark's Chief Pleas is the appointment of Lieutenant-Sénéchals to be special judges who might preside in certain circumstances, matching the modern system of judicial assistance to the Bailiff in the larger island.

The Royal Court of Guernsey has concurrent jurisdiction to attest and register Sark conveyances, and the Sénéchal of Sark takes his oath of office before it. The Royal Court appoints Sark's Greffier as Registrar of Births and Deaths, with the same functions as H.M. Greffier in Guernsey. Sark's Greffier is also customarily appointed Deputy Registrar of Marriages for the island, by Her Majesty's Greffier in Guernsey, acting in the capacity of Registrar-General for the Bailiwick. Guernsey's Customs and Immigration authorities usually appoint the Greffier of Sark to the post of Immigration Officer there.[17]

Sark's Chief Pleas continue to enjoy powers to make Ordinances in matters of public order and domestic regulation, and to seek the sanction of *Projets de Loi* by Orders in Council. Under the Law of 1951, Ordinances made by Chief Pleas are transmitted to Guernsey's Royal Court, which retains the power to annul any it finds to be unreasonable or *ultra vires*. Chief Pleas, may, however, appeal to the Privy Council in respect of such an action. The States of Guernsey may legislate for Sark, as they may for Alderney, without consent in criminal matters, and, with consent, in others.

Bailiwick-wide law

Much Bailiwick law has been brought in by single enactments, extending to all the islands. These include criminal laws, and others made with the consent of all three jurisdictions, such as, for example, *The Financial Services Commission (Bailiwick of Guernsey) Law*, 1987. In some cases, laws will apply to two jurisdictions alone, for example *The Weights and*

---

16. Order of the Sénéchal's Court 17 December 1895; action dismissed by the Royal Court 14 March 1896, and 16 June 1896; judgment of the Judicial Committee of the Privy Council 18 June 1902.
17. Beaumont, 1993 8.

Measures (Guernsey and Alderney) Law, 1991, or *The Marriages (Amendment) (Guernsey and Sark) Law*, 1994. In other instances, Guernsey's authorities will decide that the inclusion of all or any part of the rest of the Bailiwick in certain laws would be inappropriate, and will not approach other jurisdictions to seek consent. In such a situation, it remains open for one or both of the States of Alderney and Sark's Chief Pleas to seek parallel provisions for their respective islands, if they find such things to be appropriate.

In the early 1990s, Guernsey's Law Officers raised the issue of the recognition of Guernsey, Alderney, and Sark as separate jurisdictions or territories in relation to international conventions, treaties, and agreements, of the type treated in Chapter eleven, below. Correspondence resulted in an acknowledgement by the Home and Foreign and Commonwealth Offices, conveyed in a letter from the office of the Lieutenant-Governor to the Bailiff dated 9 October 1997, that, whilst each instance would continue to be treated on a case-by-case basis, and the practice would continue that each of the islands would be consulted as to their respective opinions, and that generally international instruments would be ratified in respect of the Bailiwick as a whole, when an instrument is intended to apply to one or more, but not all of the islands, these will be specified accordingly. In situations where there is autonomy between Bailiwick islands, and only one or some of these wish an instrument to be extended to it or them, and such limited ratification is appropriate, then extension is only made where requested.

Postscript: Herm and Jethou

The islands of Herm and Jethou lie alongside each other, five kilometres or so to the east of St Peter Port. Both had been let by Guernsey's Governors on short leases, limited by their terms of office, before an Order in Council of 19 May 1737 encouraged the giving of the small islands and other Crown wastes to long-term fee farm. Herm was let like this to a succession of tenants until, by a conveyance registered 17 December 1946, the States of Guernsey purchased the island outright from the Crown. Jethou was leased as a fee farm until 1846, when the Crown bought out the heirs of its late tenant, and commenced letting the island on ordinary leases. The States have been the tenants of Jethou since 26 May 1995, and sub-let the island. They also lease Herm to a tenant.[18]

A judicial decision of the Privy Council of 11 February 1837 established that Herm (and by analogy Jethou) is part and parcel of Guernsey for taxation purposes, even when not named in laws and ordinances.[19] It might be inferred from this that the same was the case with regard to legislation outside of revenue matters. It was similarly understood about that time that Acts of Parliament naming Guernsey included Herm and Jethou automatically, without mentioning them: as Advocate Peter Jeremie informed the Royal Commission appointed in 1846, as they 'are considered to be parishes of the [larger] island. Herm and Jethou are never named,' in Acts of Parliament, 'but Alderney and Sark are named, because they have a jurisdiction'.[20]

Notwithstanding the 1837 judgment, in the first half of the following century, Guernsey's authorities acted expressly to extend certain domestic laws to the smaller islands, for example under *The Island of Herm Law, (1946)* and the *Application of Existing Insular Legislation (Extension to Herm) Ordinance*, 1948. The Income Tax Laws 1920 to 1946 were extended to Herm by the former law, and today for taxation purposes the island is included in the definition of Guernsey under Section 209 of *The Income Tax (Guernsey) Law*, 1975. In contrast, in 1994 the States confirmed, for the time being, the exclusion of Jethou from the modern Guernsey Income Tax area.[21] Article 48 of the Reform Law of 1948 deemed Herm and Jethou to be parts of St Peter Port for electoral purposes, and today both are included in the electoral district of St Peter Port South.

---

18. Lihou, a tidal island off Guernsey's west coast, remains a Crown fee farm. It is presently enjoyed by the States, following a conveyance of an interest in fee farm registered 24 January 1995.

19. *Martyn, Fernie and Duncan v MacCulloch and Mansell* [1837] 1 Moo PCC 308. The judicial powers of the Guernsey courts over the two smaller islands have never been questioned.

20. Commission 1846, 1848 108, and cf. 187.

21. *Billet d'État* xvi 1994 (27 July) and resolution thereon. The *Billet* did not seek the States' active confirmation of the state of affairs with regard to tax, but expressed the Advisory and Finance Committee's view that the exemption should continue, and the subsequent resolution contains no indication of any opposition to it. Whether the States could in any case by mere resolution vary a judicial decision of the Privy Council is doubtful to say the least.

9. Guernsey and the United Kingdom

As mentioned in the introduction to this survey, and illustrated throughout, Guernsey's modern constitution is rooted in Anglo-Norman history. The Channel Islands were integrated administratively into the Duchy of Normandy possibly in the tenth, and certainly in the eleventh century. The Duchy became closely associated with the English Crown following the Battle of Hastings. Soon after the French king conquered Normandy in 1204, the Islands returned to the dominion of the English king, who ruled them in his capacity as Duke of Normandy until, by the Treaty of Paris of 1259, Henry III formally abandoned this title. The Treaty also confirmed the king's right to the Islands.[1] In 1254, Henry had granted them, with much else, to his son, 'the Lord Edward' (the future Edward I) 'in such manner that the said lands ... may never be separated from the Crown and that no one, by reason of this grant made to the said Edward may have any claim to the said lands ... but that they should remain to the Kings of England in their entirety for ever'. Thus the Islands were annexed to the Crown, and the legitimate King of England came to be the legally recognised ruler of the Channel Islands, although they have never been incorporated into the English, still less the United, Kingdom. Although the King of England surrendered the title of Duke of Normandy by the treaty of 1259, he still ruled the Islands in just that capacity, continuing to observe their established laws, liberties, usages and customs, as confirmed by the successive charters referred to above.[2] This, then, is the origin of the Channel Islands' status as 'Crown Dependencies'.

---

1. Le Patourel, 1974 453.
2. Loveridge, 1974 393.

The Royal Prerogative

The origins of the Sovereign's prerogative powers in the Channel Islands lie in this Anglo-Norman context. Certain, not altogether well defined, powers rested with the Dukes of Normandy. As mentioned in Chapter seven, at some point, possibly in the early eleventh century, these were limited in the Islands in some respects, whether by the Duke's grace or for more compelling reasons. Of the prerogative powers that remain, sovereign responsibility for the Islands' defence and international relations are relatively well defined, although not quite as clearly in the case of the latter as the former. So, too, is the sovereign right of dispensing justice, including the granting of free pardons, and otherwise as exercised by bodies including Guernsey's Royal Court and the Judicial Committee of the Privy Council. Less clear is the scope of the Crown's prerogative in ecclesiastical affairs, and, especially in the modern democratic context, the extent of any residual sovereign power, exercised in Council, to legislate without consent for the Bailiwick, or to refuse or delay registration of, or modify, legislation promoted by the islands' legitimate representative institutions.[3]

The Lieutenant-Governor

Following the loss of Normandy, the English king usually appointed what in English was called a 'Warden' or 'Keeper' (*Custos* in Latin, *Gardien* in French) to represent his interests in the Channel Islands, overseeing defence, administering justice, collecting revenues, and organizing assizes.[4] No single Wardens serving both the Bailiwicks of Guernsey and Jersey were appointed after 1473.[5] The office increasingly came to be known as that of 'Captain' or 'Governor' and in 1618 the Privy Council decreed as respects Jersey that the latter style should

---

3. Cf de Smith and Brazier, 1998 60 n.63, citing *Campbell v Hall* [1774] 1 Cowp. 774. See also Roberts-Wray, 1966 157–163. The latter work conveniently reprints extracts of a report of *Campbell v Hall* at pages 929–33.

4. Le Patourel, 1937 40–42.

5. Richard Harliston was 'captain in chief' of Guernsey and Jersey 1473–86, though in 1478 separate captains were appointed to both islands, under him: Thornton, 2004 46.

prevail.[6] In Guernsey other usages fell out of fashion at about the same time, or a little before.

Governors, often resident in England, usually appointed lieutenants, resident in Guernsey, to oversee affairs. By the nineteenth century, the governorship itself had become a sinecure, and the office was abolished in 1835 after the death of the Governor, General Sir William Keppel, on 11 December 1834.[7] The practice of appointing Lieutenant-Governors continued, as it does today. Some of the royal revenues, such as parts of Crown rents and manorial dues received, which had once been enjoyed by Governors, were granted piecemeal to meet particular insular needs, for example for maintaining the prison, until by virtue of the Jersey and Guernsey (Financial Provisions) Act 1947, and *The Lieutenant Governor (Salary and Official Expenses) Law*, 1948, the whole amount then still collected was assigned to the States, in consideration of them taking on financial responsibility for the Crown establishment in Guernsey.

Lieutenant-Governors normally hold office for a term of five years, being appointed by the Queen on the recommendation of the Lord Chancellor in his capacity as Privy Councillor with special responsibility for the Channel Islands (formerly the Home Secretary did this, and, at the proposed abolition of the office of Lord Chancellor, presumably in future the Secretary of State for Constititutional Affairs – providing that office is not itself restructured or redesignated – will take on responsibility). The Lieutenant-Governor is Her Majesty's personal representative in the Bailiwick of Guernsey and impartial advisor to her there, although as long ago as 24 September 1957 the Home Office, in a letter located by Dr Luke Le Rendu, noted that application was never made to the Lieutenant-Governors of Guernsey and Jersey for impartial advice, nor was it volunteered.[8] The Lieutenant-Governor's office is the official channel of communication between the Bailiwick's authorities and the United Kingdom government. He submits citations recommending honours and awards, in consultation with the Bailiff (who as civic head of the community receives recommendations from the public, island organisations, and suchlike) and represents the Queen on official occasions. Candidates for the post are expected to have a record of distinguished Crown service, diplomatic talents, and a willingness to be

---

6. Bois, 1972 20.
7. Tupper, 1876 116.
8. Le Rendu, 1999 37. For an earlier period, see Stevens Cox, 2003.

involved in a wide variety of community activities.[9] The Lieutenant-Governor also issues passports and has certain statutory duties, chiefly relating to matters of immigration and national security, under the Immigration Act 1971, extended to Guernsey by the Immigration (Guernsey) Order 1993, and *The Terrorism and Crime (Bailiwick of Guernsey) Law*, 2002. He has responsibilities for shipping licences in the islands of Alderney and Sark, under *The Alderney and Sark (Licencing of Vessels) Law*, 1951, and in Guernsey acts for the Crown on the appointment of rectors, and appoints Her Majesty's Sergeant, two directors of Elizabeth College and, on its Board's recommendation, the Principal, and also nominates two members of the Priaulx Library Council.

The Lieutenant-Governor was also historically Commander in Chief in the Bailiwick of Guernsey. Between the Medieval and Modern eras the islands' fortifications were garrisoned, and their localities defended by militias. The last garrison was withdrawn in 1939, and the Royal Guernsey Militia suspended in January 1940. It was not to be revived.[10] Of the major fortifications, the Crown transferred Castle Cornet to the States in 1948, and they acquired Fort George from the War Department in 1959. The Lieutenant-Governor does retain powers of requisition for the military use of L'Ancresse Common, under Section 20 of the *Ordonnance relative aux Communes de la Valle*, 1932. This power has not been resorted to in living memory, a circumstance, were they only to know it, of satisfaction to residents, other commoners, and the golfing community alike.

The *Précepte d'Assize* (1441) refers to the presentation by Governors of their commissions to the Bailiff and Jurats, and the oath they took on the Holy Gospels before them, which mentioned their obligations to maintain the Bailiwick's defences, the loyalty of the islanders, and their liberties, usages and established customs.[11] The oath remained substantially in that form in the seventeenth century.[12] Today Lieutenant-Governors still swear on the Gospels before the Royal Court to maintain and defend Guernsey and its dependencies 'both in the spiritual and temporal', to keep and preserve the castles (a now otiose provision, as

---

9. *Sunday Times*, 1999.
10. Cruickshank, 1975 23; Parks, 1992 24.
11. De Sausmarez, 1934 133–34, 146.
12. 'Warburton', 1822 32–33.

just mentioned), to 'keep and maintain in like manner the commons and inhabitants of this isle and its dependencies in their true allegiance and fidelity to Her ... Majesty', and to 'preserve and support the said inhabitants of this said island and its dependencies in their rights, liberties and privileges and ancient customs, and ... likewise [to] maintain the ordinances for the time being in force'. The oath administered by the Royal Court to the Lieutenant-Governor concludes with the words 'if peradventure you should act, or do anything contrary to the said privileges, ancient customs and ordinances that you will at all times upon conference with the Bailiff and Jurats and their pointing it out to you, redress the same in everything that shall be meet and reasonable'.[13]

Her Majesty's Receiver General

The Crown office of Receiver can be traced back to the early thirteen-hundreds. From the middle of the century he was responsible for submitting to the Exchequer, sometimes *via* the Warden, accounts of the king's rents and other income, and expenditure on things such as salaries, defence and charity.[14] The Receiver General, as the officer is now known, is appointed by royal warrant, holding office during Her Majesty's pleasure, and functioning under the authority of the United Kingdom Department for Constitutional Affairs. The activity required of the Receiver General was successively diminished in the twentieth century by the assignment of Crown revenues to the States in consideration of the transfer of responsibility for the costs of the Crown establishment to them in the nineteen-forties, as stated above, and the abandonment of the uneconomic collection of minor manorial dues in the early nineteen-eighties, and later *treizième* too, under *The Feudal Dues (General Abolition of Congé) (Guernsey) Law*, 2002. Since 1985 the position of Receiver General has been occupied by successive holders of the post of Her Majesty's Procureur. Residual duties include negotiation for the sale or letting of Crown lands (and participation as a lessor in respect of leaseholds, such as that of Jethou, as described in the last chapter), dealing with escheated and *bona vacantia* properties, foreshores and other manorial possessions (usually managed, by arrangement, by

---

13. 'Ordinances' in the oath must refer to all legislation in force.
14. Le Patourel, 1937 63–64, 86–87.

the States' Environment Department), directing the preparation of annual accounts in respect of Crown revenues for approval by the Lieutenant-Governor and H.M. Receiver General, and presiding over Chief Pleas dinners.

Guernsey and United Kingdom Government Departments

From its creation in 1782, the United Kingdom Government Department dealing with relations with the Channel Islands was the Home Office, and the Secretary of State for the Home Department, in the capacity of a Privy Councillor, the minister with responsibility. In June 2001, however, as part of a wider government reorganisation, this connection was severed and responsibility transferred to the Lord Chancellor. When the office of Lord Chancellor is eventually abolished, as announced by the Prime Minister on 11 June 2003, it is anticipated that the Secretary of State for Constitutional Affairs will take on this role. The United Kingdom Department for Constitutional Affairs, as the Lord Chancellor's Department has already been renamed, is the main channel of communication between the States and the United Kingdom Government. It acts on behalf of the Bailiwick at Whitehall by liaising with other departments, and representing the interests of the islands. Direct links also exist with other Government Departments, with these providing a variety of advice and services to Departments of the States. They may, for example, be invited to comment on legislation that is intended, or – in less detail – on measures passed by the States awaiting Privy Council sanction.[15]

Royal Commissions and the like

Sir Edward Coke (1552–1634) in the fourth part of his *Institutes*, cited an attempt in 1368 to bring a Jersey case of trespass before the English Court of King's Bench. The judgment included these words:

> ... And since the matter aforesaid cannot be determined in this court, because the Jurats of the said island cannot come here [to appear] before the Justices, nor are they bound to do so by law, nor may any other matter arising in the said island be determined otherwise than by

---

15. Lord Chancellor's Department, 2002 para 30.

the custom of the said island, therefore let the whole record of this matter be sent to the Lord King's Chancery, so that his commission may be addressed to such persons as he pleases, to hear and determine the matter aforesaid in the said island according to the custom of the said island.[16]

From this judgment, Coke concluded 'that albeit the kings writ runneth not into these isles, yet his commission under the great seal doth, but the commissioners must judge according to the laws and custome of these isles',[17] a rule that has consistently marked not only the proceedings of royal commissions, but is also one that was set out in commissions to justices itinerant sent to the Islands in the medieval period, and which is observed by the Judicial Committee of the Privy Council to this day.

In the latter half of the sixteenth century, several Royal Commissions were charged with functions relating to ecclesiastical, legal, and property issues in Guernsey, notably those of 1563, 1579 and 1597. Another Commission, created in 1607, heard a wide range of complaints and made orders and judgments. Its findings, on the whole, were endorsed by an Order in Council of 30 June 1608.[18] A Royal Commission appointed in 1815 was similarly authorised to make judgments in certain private lawsuits and investigate matters relating to insolvency. Its findings in the latter regard, ultimately, after consultation and modification, were embodied in an Order in Council of 13 May 1823.[19] The last Royal Commission investigating an aspect of Guernsey's law and constitution as a major part of its agenda was that appointed on 16 May 1846 to enquire into the state of the criminal law in the Channel Islands.[20] The Commission reported in 1848, with certain recommendations. Some of these, although by no means the most ambitious, were introduced, mostly by means of locally generated *Projets de Loi*, giving rise to Orders in Council that were promulgated 1849–61.[21]

The twentieth century saw a move away from the employment of full Royal Commissions to examine Channel Island affairs, to that of the investigative powers of specially formed committees of the Privy

---

16. Coke, 1817 286, translated from the Latin, Le Patourel, 1962 208.
17. Coke, 1817 286.
18. Eagleston, 1949 103–04.
19. Commission 1815, 1823.
20. Commission 1846, 1848.
21. Hocart, 1988 56–57.

Council. The first of these was created in 1925, in connection with the Imperial Contribution affair, discussed later in this chapter. In 1946, both the Guernsey and Jersey States considered the reform of their islands' respective constitutions and judicial systems. Another Committee of the Privy Council was created, by Order of 4 June 1946.[22] In Guernsey, the outcome of the local initiative and the report of the Committee of 1947 was the Reform Law of 1948.

The Royal Commission on the Constitution 1969–73 was appointed to consider, amongst other things, whether changes were desirable in the constitutional and economic relations between the Channel Islands and the United Kingdom, especially with regard to the application to the Islands of international treaties. After taking evidence from the Channel Islands' authorities and United Kingdom Government Departments, the Commission, in the so-called 'Kilbrandon Report', recommended a strengthening of consultative procedures, whilst strongly asserting that powers of last resort in the international relations and good government of the Islands rested with the United Kingdom Government.[23] The Commission's conclusions were never altogether accepted in the Islands, and in today's post-colonial democratic context appear particularly dated and questionable.[24]

In January 1998 the Home Secretary commissioned Andrew Edwards, a former Treasury Civil Servant, to review with the authorities of

---

22.   Privy Council, 1947; Hocart, 1988 126–27.
23.   Commission 1969–73, 1973 407, 465. The reference to 'good government' was echoed in a question raised by Baroness Strange, in the House of Lords on 3 May 2000, of the circumstances in which the United Kingdom Government might introduce prerogative legislation, when she asked Her Majesty's Government, 'Whether they are responsible for the 'good government' of the Crown Dependencies; if so, how they define 'good government'; and in what circumstances they would intervene to that end in the affairs of the Dependencies'. Lord Bach, Parliamentary Secretary in the Lord Chancellor's Department, replied for the Government, by written answer, that 'The Crown is ultimately responsible for the good government of the Crown Dependencies. This means that, in the circumstances of a grave breakdown or failure in the administration of justice or civil order, the residual prerogative power of the Crown could be used to intervene in the internal affairs of the Channel Islands and the Isle of Man. It is unhelpful to the relationship between Her Majesty's Government and the Islands to speculate about the hypothetical and highly unlikely circumstances in which such intervention might take place.' (Hansard, 2000 col. WA 180, cf. Lord Chancellor's Department, 2002 para. 15).
24.   Eg. see the opinions expressed in Bailhache, 2001, Bailhache, 2002, Jowell, 2001.

Guernsey, Jersey, and the Isle of Man their systems, practices and laws regulating banking and other financial services, financial crime, and company registration. The review was a United Kingdom Government initiative, although the islands' authorities were consulted closely in the preparation of the report of November 1998, entitled the *Review of Financial Regulation in the Crown Dependencies*. Whilst the Edwards' Report reached a variety of conclusions, and stimulated some development of regulation, generally its findings were that the islands' systems work well.[25] It is now recognised that the United Kingdom Government, with advance knowledge of a number of international reviews, foresaw the need to ensure that the Crown Dependencies would have in place in good time all necessary laws and regulations to emerge favourably from such scrutiny.

The Privy Council Committee for the Affairs of Jersey and Guernsey

The role of the Judicial Committee of the Privy Council, created in 1833, in hearing appeals from Guernsey was described in Chapter five. Between the sixteenth and nineteenth centuries, the Privy Council was also in a wider sense a vehicle for the creation of Bailiwick law, issuing directions, answering petitions, settling disputes, and making peremptory orders. From the mid nineteenth century it has considered petitions from the islands transmitting *Projets de Loi* submitted for Royal assent, embodying them in Orders in Council, as it still does today.

An Order was passed on 31 January 1668 regulating the committees of the Privy Council. Another Order in Council followed on 12 February 1668, creating standing committees. One of these was charged with wide-ranging responsibilities, including the treatment of matters relating to Guernsey and Jersey. Here lies the origin of the Committee of the Privy Council for the Affairs of Jersey and Guernsey. The quorum created in 1668 was three, and this remains the case with the current Committee, which was established by an Order in Council of 22 February 1952. Petitions from the States of Guernsey for the approval of *Projets de Loi* are submitted to the Committee, which makes a report that is read at the Board of the Privy Council, attended by Her Majesty the Queen, certain Ministers in their capacity as Privy Councillors, and the Clerk of the

---

25. Edwards, 1998.

Council. No deliberations take place at this point, the Queen simply giving formal approval to an Order embodying the law. On occasions when Her Majesty is not in the United Kingdom, power to signify approval is delegated under the Regency Acts 1937 to 1952 to between two and six Privy Councillors, named from time to time by Letters Patent.

Even in the period when Orders in Council were made regularly without consultation, the Channel Islands' authorities were not slow to protest when they perceived their laws to have been infringed or threatened, and would suspend registration in such circumstances (the view being that registration of an Order in the island – as also of an Act of Parliament – was necessary before it could take proper effect). Some examples follow.

In 1708, Guernsey's Royal Court refused to register Orders in Council relating to the powers of customs officers, on the grounds that they were incompatible with the island's rights. A delegation was sent to London, and the Orders were withdrawn and substitutions made. A similar problem arose with regard to an Order of 13 February 1767, on the same issue. Again, a deputation protested. On this occasion, however, representations appear to have been wholly unsuccessful, and the Royal Court registered the Order on 21 November 1767, although not without recording its objections at the same time.[26] In 1776, in the circumstances of a dispute between one of the advocates and the Bailiff, the Court delayed the registration of two Orders in Council concerning the affair, in order to approach the Council. However, following receipt of a stiff letter from the latter, registration immediately took place.[27] Registration was also delayed after the Royal Court's receipt of an Order in Council dated 1 March 1849 concerning *impôt* (duty on liquor) which it was felt impinged on the States' right to determine the use of their own revenues. After consulting with the States, the Court registered the Order on 24 March 1849, with a note to the effect that the States might wish to approach the Privy Council to seek its modification. Probably the last occasion when the Royal Court found it necessary to delay registration occurred in connection with an Order in Council of 4 February 1869 concerning funds for the roads. The Court consulted the States as to

---

26. Hocart, 1988 17–18.
27. Commission 1846, 1848 108–09.

whether they wished to make representations to the Privy Council, and on receiving a negative response, registered the Order, on 1 May 1869.[28]

A greater degree of consultation and developing convention together mean that the Royal Court has not had cause to delay the registration of original Orders in Council (as opposed to those merely conveying Acts of Parliament, to which we shortly turn) in the like manner since the mid nineteenth century.

Guernsey and Parliament

The extent of the power of Parliament to legislate for the Channel Islands, particularly in domestic and taxation matters, has been much debated. The fourth part of Coke's *Institutes* simply states that the Channel Islands 'are not bound by our acts of parliament, unlesse they be specially named',[29] and both before and after Coke's time a variety of Parliamentary legislation extended to the Islands.[30] However, as just seen with regard to Orders in Council, when it has been perceived that this has infringed Guernsey's ancient constitution, reaction has often been passionate.

In 1440, the English government raised a tax on aliens, and the definition of these included Channel Islanders. The latter were not slow to protest at this, and three years later, when a tax was again raised, they were exempted.[31] The Act for Chantries Collegiate, of 1547, which sought to close down religious guilds and confiscate their revenues, purported to extend throughout all 'the Realm of England ... [and] other the King's Dominions'. Guernsey's Royal Court took strenuous action, to the point of subversion, in avoiding English intentions for the island's religious life.[32] Dr Heyting found no similar reaction recorded with regard to 'An Act for prohibiting the planting, setting or sowing of tobacco in England or Ireland', of 1660, extending to Guernsey and Jersey.[33] Yet, since cultivation in the islands had already been banned by

---

28. Hocart, 1988 48, 52.
29. Coke, 1817, 287; Cf. Anon., 1837 373
30. Cf. Ogier, 1996 7.
31. Thornton, 2004 21.
32. Ogier, 1996 45–50.
33. Heyting, 1977 75.

an Order in Council of 6 January 1631, protests would have been pointless.

Registration

When the issue of the necessity of registering Acts of Parliament in the Islands in order to give them legal effect arose with regard to the extension of the Navigation Act to Jersey, in 1698, the English position was established in a memorandum of Sir Thomas Trevor (1658–1730) Attorney General for England. His opinion, very likely developing what was to be read in Coke, was 'that the registering of any act of parliament made in England, wherein the island is expressly named, is not necessary in point of law to make it obligatory there, and such registry is only for the convenience of the island, that they may have notice of what acts are made in England to bind them'.

'An Act for the more effectual collecting in Great Britain and Ireland, and other parts of His Majesty's dominions, the duties granted for the support of the royal hospital at Greenwich', of 1729, novelly required Guernsey's mariners to make monthly payments, and it met stiff resistance in the island, where the States detected encroachment upon chartered rights. A delegation was sent to England, and George II petitioned.[34] Notwithstanding this effort, the outcome did not favour the Guernsey authorities, and the Royal Court finally registered the Act on 4 October 1731. The Order in Council of 1 July 1731 conveying it, apparently for reasons of convenience, and not in modification of Trevor's opinion, set down that

> ... for the future whenever any act shall be passed in the Parliament of Great Britain, relating to the said islands of Guernsey and Jersey printed copies of such acts shall be transmitted by the Clerk of His Majesty's Privy Council as soon as conveniently may be to the Royal Courts of the said islands, signifying to them at the same time His Majesty's pleasure to register and publish the said Acts, and cause the same to be carried into due execution.

---

34. Lee, 1907 163–64, 166–68.

In 1805, the intention to extend a proposed 'Act for the Better Prevention of Smuggling' became known in the Channel Islands. The States petitioned the House of Lords, requesting to

... be heard and examined ... in defence and support of the chartered rights, immunities and privileges of the said island of Guernsey, and against all such parts of the said Act as may affect the inhabitants of the said island of Guernsey, or which may alter, impeach or affect the ancient and established constitution of the said island ... and that the said Act may not pass into a law, as it now stands.[35]

A Committee of the whole House heard counsel for Guernsey, the matter was debated, and the Act was approved, by a majority of nineteen to six.[36] The Lords of the Committee for the affairs of Guernsey and Jersey had considered Trevor's opinion of 1698, and concurred with it, as the Council's Order of 7 May 1806, directing registration, spells out:

Upon the whole their lordships are of opinion that as the act in question is binding by its own force and there exists no power of suspending its execution either in whole or in part the delay in registering it can have no other effect than to deprive the inhabitants of Guernsey of that usual notification of its provisions which was meant to be given them by the registration directed by your Majesty's before mentioned Order in Council ... [of 15 August 1805, transmitting the Act]

The king on the advice of the Privy Council thereupon peremptorily required the Royal Court to carry into execution the Order in Council directing the disputed Act's registration.

It appears from the Greffe register that in the next decade or so, in the spirit of the Order of 1806, there began the practice of qualifying transmissions of Acts with an accompanying notice 'that the said Act be registered and published in the island of Guernsey, not as being essential to its operation therein; but that Her [or His] Majesty's subjects in the Bailiwick may have notice of the said Act having passed and that they are bound thereby'.[37]

---

35. Anon., 1837–38 369.
36. Duncan, 1841 250–57.
37. Cf. Jacob, 1830 341; Commission 1846, 1848 108.

The Merchant Shipping Act of 1854, as originally drafted, provided that the Channel Islands' authorities should act as registrars of shipping within their respective jurisdictions, that the Board of Trade should introduce a particular toll on shipping, extending to the Islands, and that Trinity House should have power over certain buoys etc., hitherto the responsibility of the States. The Royal Court and the States objected to this on the grounds that it represented an intervention in domestic affairs by bodies other than the Privy Council. The matter was resolved by the final statute providing that lighthouse tolls should not be levied without the States' consent, nor the jurisdiction of Trinity House extend to local waters, unless provided for by Order in Council.[38] Such an Order in Council was duly registered by Guernsey's Royal Court on 18 November 1854.

On the transmission of the Burial Laws Amendment Act 1880 to Guernsey's Royal Court for registration, the question arose as to whether this similarly represented interference in Guernsey's domestic affairs. The Royal Court therefore deferred registration and consulted the States, who voted that the Act did encroach on their right to legislate in local matters, and resolved to make representations to the Privy Council. No response to communications was received, and in 1881, when alternative local legislation was proposed and found to be still less attractive, the States asked the Royal Court to proceed with registration of the statute. Some States' members chose to see the Council's lack of response as a victory for their standpoint.[39]

The Civil Aviation Act 1946 gave the state-owned airline passenger carriers the monopoly of scheduled services. It had been the United Kingdom Government's intention to apply the Act directly to the Channel Islands, but following representations from Guernsey and Jersey, an agreement was reached that the Act should be extended by way of an Order in Council. After States' representations had been made, The Civil Aviation Act (Extension to the Channel Islands) Order 1947 was duly prepared and registered in both islands. Under the Order and the Act, the islands had to submit to the domination of communications between the islands and United Kingdom, and the

---

38. Heyting, 1977 105; Hocart, 1988 86. Modern arrangements with Trinity House are the subject of Section 203 of *The Merchant Shipping (Bailiwick of Guernsey) Law*, 2002.
39. Hocart, 1988 87.

islands and Europe, by the publicly-owned corporations or their associates. It was conceded, however, that Guernsey and Jersey should retain ownership and control of their respective airports, and might licence airlines operating between the islands themselves. The United Kingdom Government's policy was publicly regarded in Guernsey and Jersey with concern, and whilst a compromise was achieved, the islands by no means got their own way. The current Civil Aviation Act, of 1982, which was created against a rather different social and political background from that existing in 1946, was extended to Guernsey by an Order in Council registered 27 April 1987, only after consultation between Whitehall and the island's authorities had taken place. This matches modern procedures, and the United Kingdom Government *Guide to Government Business involving the Channel Islands and the Isle of Man* of 2002 notes that 'For an Act to extend otherwise than by an Order in Council is now very unusual. The Insular Authorities would be fully consulted in the rare event that the former approach was under consideration'.[40]

Financial Contributions

On two occasions in the twentieth century, United Kingdom Governments sought direct financial contributions from the Channel Islands. These requests raised some of the same constitutional issues as the legislation just examined. The first of the incidents is known, by the few who discuss such things, as the 'Imperial Contribution' affair. By a letter dated 30 January 1923, addressed to the Bailiff and the States, William Clive Bridgeman (1864–1935) the Home Secretary, without warning invited Guernsey's authorities to consider making an annual payment to the United Kingdom Exchequer. The stated motivation for the request was the serious condition of British finances after the Great War, as set out in a Treasury memorandum that was perceived in Guernsey (which was itself reeling after the loss of hundreds of men in combat) as 'amazing', containing inaccuracies, and to demonstrate a 'palpable ignorance of local conditions'.[41] The States appointed a Committee under the presidency of Sir Havilland Walter de Sausmarez, Bart. (1861–1941, Bailiff 1922–29) which first reported its opinion that although the

---

40. Lord Chancellor's Department, 2002 para. 36.
41. De Sausmarez, 1930 11, 70, 12.

request was not a tax, there was a danger of the creation of a permanent obligation. The Committee suggested the matter might be resolved by an offer to the United Kingdom Government to take on liability for the pensions of former island servicemen and their dependants. After debate, the States deferred consideration for four months. An enlarged Committee then produced a second report, in January 1924, suggesting that the payment of pensions would be too onerous, and recommending instead a one-off gift of £220,000. This offer was conveyed to Whitehall the following month. It went unacknowledged. In March 1925 the Privy Council constituted its own Committee, which, under the Duke of Atholl, was to report on the affair. It visited Guernsey in October, and the States rejected its suggestion of an annual contribution of £75,000 the following month. The Privy Council Committee's report, signed on 29 January 1926, proposed that such a sum should be paid for one hundred years, and also asserted, although without going deeply into the constitutional question, that Parliament could impose this obligation as a tax, if necessary. On 8 September 1926 the States agreed to repeat its earlier proposal of a one-off payment, and to offer assistance with regard to the alleged presence of English tax avoiders in Guernsey: a subject that, not for the last time, was exercising British minds. After a debate on the subject at a States' meeting of 4 August 1927, these proposals were accepted by the United Kingdom Government, but never implemented, because the relevant Bill failed in Parliament, probably due to Dominion objections. On 1 January 1928, the sum of £220,000, by way of a gift, was paid.[42] Although the Imperial Contribution affair raised difficult issues for the States, its resolution by compromise, and its settlement by considerably less than a commitment to pay £7,500,000, as had been proposed, avoided more serious constitutional conflict.[43]

In 1984, the Secretary of State for the Home Department, apparently stimulated by Jersey's gift to H.M. Government two years earlier of £5,000,000 towards the costs of retaking and rehabilitating the

---

42. Hocart, 1988 111–13.
43. One (extra-Parliamentary) outcome, agreed at a conference held at the U.K. Treasury 14–15 July 1927, was the strengthening of the Royal Court's requirement, first made in 1923, that the Law Officers of the Crown, prior to the consent of the Royal Court to the registration of a limited company, should approve its objects and constitution: de Sausmarez, 1930 57–64. The Law Officers' visa remains a necessity today.

Falkland Islands,[44] raised the question of a contribution from the Channel Islands towards the cost of defence expenditure and international representation undertaken by the United Kingdom on the Islands' behalf. Whilst he acknowledged the special circumstances of the Channel Islands, and the nature of their ties to the United Kingdom, the request was to an extent regarded in Guernsey as a threat to the constitutional *status quo*, recalling the Imperial Contribution affair, and indeed many of the arguments advanced in connection with that affair were quoted in a *Billet d'État* on the request, considered at a States' meeting of 27 November 1985. A compromise was reached, in a manner again recalling the earlier difficulty, with the States in 1987 undertaking to save the United Kingdom expenditure by themselves maintaining Alderney's breakwater, contributing to the upkeep of the Royal Naval Port Headquarters in Guernsey (now redundant), paying over to Her Majesty's Government fees charged for the issue of passports in Guernsey, and meeting certain expenses incurred by the Government, including those in respect of legal advice, and awards by international courts of compensation for injuries sustained in Guernsey. The Home Secretary, for his part, confirmed that acceptance of the offer did not change the constitutional relationship between Her Majesty's Government and Guernsey. Once again, honour on both sides was satisfied, and what was perceived in some quarters to be a threat to the constitution avoided.

An invitation to further study

Foregoing paragraphs have shown that English and United Kingdom Governments have from time to time reviewed island institutions, and requested money of their citizens (even though they are not represented in the United Kingdom Parliament).[45] Governments have also asserted a perceived right to extend parliamentary legislation to the Channel Islands without their consent, even, although exceptionally, in the purely domestic field. Registration of Orders in Council and Acts of Parliament

---

44. The States of Guernsey, under a resolution of 26 October 1983, donated £100,000 direct to the Falkland Islands' government, towards the cost of providing sheltered accommodation for the Islands' elderly.
45. Cf. Blackstone, 1825 101 on Ireland, and note also, more generally, the causes of the American Revolution.

has been regarded by English administrations as desirable, but not necessary to give them effect. The Islands' response has often been to oppose such opinions, and to find such interference frankly illegal, according to their laws. Modern convention, and democratic and constitutional ideas support such a position.[46]

Any fuller discussion is out of place here: Mr Hocart commented in 1988 that the 'full story of the relationship between the Channel Islands and the United Kingdom calls for a separate study', and the present writer can only echo that.[47] Pending the realisation of such a bold venture, the reader is referred to the various views of Professor Albert Venn Dicey, QC, (1835–1922), those expressed in the Kilbrandon Report, the contribution of Professor John Finnis, FBA, to Halsbury's *Laws of England*, Professor Rodney Brazier's edition of de Smith's *Constitutional and Administrative Law*, and the Jersey perspectives supplied by William Bailhache, QC, and Professor Jeffrey Jowell, QC, as set out in their works, listed in the bibliography.[48]

---

46.   Jowell, 2001 273–74 says of the Channel Islands that 'The United Kingdom has never enacted laws for their domestic affairs without their consent'. Whilst on the evidence presented above Professor Jowell's view is to be questioned, it would be an error to hold that Parliament might still unilaterally enact laws for the domestic affairs of the Channel Islands. Professor Brazier has succinctly stated as much: ' . . . the Government would not sponsor legislation which flagrantly violated a constitutional convention restricting the territorial ambit or subject-matter of legislative competence. It would not initiate legislation intended to encroach on the autonomy of an independent Commonwealth country or, for example, to impose changes in the laws of the Channel Islands on purely domestic matters.' (de Smith and Brazier, 1998 98), cf. Lord Chancellor's Department, 2002 para. 28.

47.   Hocart, 1988 ix.

48.   Cf., with regard to Finnis, Le Cras, 1839 (with Kilbrandon, Professor Finnis' main authority) and with regard to Bailhache and Jowell, Haldane, 2001, Le Quesne, 1992, and Swinfen, 1975.

10. Guernsey and Europe

On 2 May 1967, Harold Wilson, the Prime Minister, announced in the House of Commons the United Kingdom Government's intention to apply for membership of the European Economic Community. The following day, a Home Office letter formally conveyed the news to Guernsey's Lieutenant-Governor. The letter, which was published in a *Billet d'État* considered at a States' meeting held on 31 May 1967, pulled no punches:

> The Secretary of State [for the Home Department] is aware that the Insular Authorities have already given anxious consideration to the implications for the island of entry into the Community alongside the United Kingdom. As they will know, Article 227(4) of the Treaty of Rome provides that the Treaty shall apply to the European territories for whose external relations a Member State is responsible. If, therefore, the United Kingdom were to accede to the Treaty, it would apply to Guernsey, unless it were possible to negotiate some modification of the Article in its application to Guernsey. The chances of securing such a modification must be considered remote; but in any event it must be questionable whether such arrangements would be desirable, because, if Guernsey were excluded, the island would have to face the Common External Tariff that would need to be erected against it by the United Kingdom and the other Community countries. From its present position of enjoyment of a protected market in the United Kingdom it would at one bound be faced with tariff barriers that could amount to virtual exclusion from the markets of both the United Kingdom and a large part of the European continent.

The States faced a dilemma. As the Home Office letter indicated, if Guernsey chose not to join the Community, the island's economy, which at the time was dominated by the horticultural trade, could have suffered severely, due to the imposition of a tariff on exports to the United Kingdom. However, as set out in a report of the States' European Free Trade Association and Economic Community Committee, considered by a States' meeting held on 25 October 1967, if the island were to join the Community, there would still be a threat to the economy, due to the Community's internal free trade principles. This would be accompanied by a loss of autonomy in legislative affairs, although the island would not be represented in Community institutions. Existing immigration controls and housing regulations might also have been affected.[1]

Independence was one available course. On 28 October 1966, the Home Secretary, Roy Jenkins, had suggested that for the Channel Islands to remain outside the Community, 'would be a possible position' for them to take

> ... if they so wish. If they wished to take up such a position, it might be regarded as a little isolated to be not part of a unit which both France and England were part of, but independence means independence. Independence means to right to take independent decisions and in the event of Great Britain becoming part of the Common Market ... it would be a matter for the Channel Islands to decide what they thought was in their best interests.[2]

Another course was the obtaining of special conditions for the Bailiwick, and notwithstanding the pessimism of the Home Office letter of 3 May 1967, the States of Guernsey brought the difficulties to the notice of the United Kingdom Government, requesting an examination of the possibility of excluding the Bailiwick from certain provisions of the Treaty of Rome of 1957, particularly those relating to tax, agriculture, and immigration.

It turned out that the European Community rejected the United Kingdom's 1967 request to join it. However, when in 1971 the application was revived, the issues for the Bailiwick were clear, and preparations were in hand. Consultations between the islands' authorities and the United Kingdom Government took place, and representations were made to the Community. At a meeting attended by members of the States of Guernsey, the States of Alderney, and Sark's Chief Pleas, held on 19 November 1971, the United Kingdom Government's chief negotiator, Geoffrey Rippon, spelled out the proposed arrangements to which the Community had agreed. He was able to reveal to the Bailiwick

---

1. Cf. Vibert, 1967 5–10; Vibert, 1991 ch. 19.
2. Quoted, Vibert, 1967 4.

legislatures that: 'Under the proposals your fiscal autonomy has been guaranteed. I can say quite categorically that there will be no question of your having to apply a value-added tax or any part of Community policy on taxation', and referred to 'a choice of accepting or rejecting the terms that have been negotiated', adding that it was not for him 'to try to influence you in that decision, because the decision is yours, and yours alone. I can only say to you today that I know what my decision would be'.[3] The States of Guernsey concurred, voting unanimously to accept the negotiated terms at their meeting held on 15 December 1971. These terms were subsequently embodied in Protocol No. 3 on the Channel Islands and the Isle of Man of the Treaty of Accession of the United Kingdom to the European Community, signed on 22 January 1972.

Although Guernsey is neither a separate Member State nor an Associate Member of the European Community, Article 1 of Protocol No. 3 placed the Channel Islands within the Common Customs Area and the Common External Tariff of the European Community. This applied Community rules on customs matters to the Islands, also allowing them to make physical exports to Community countries without tariff barriers intervening. Article 2 confirmed the rights enjoyed by Channel Islanders in the United Kingdom, although it excluded such persons from the benefit of Community provisions relating to the free movement of persons and services. Article 3 applied aspects of the European Atomic Energy Community (Euratom) Treaty to the Islands. Article 4 provided that Island authorities should treat Community natural and legal persons equally. Article 5 provided that in the event of difficulties arising in the application of the Protocol, the European Commission should make proposals for safeguard measures to the Council. The sixth and last Article set out a definition that had the effect of applying the Protocol's terms to all Channel Islanders other than those who were 'born, adopted, naturalised or registered in the United Kingdom' or had a parent or grandparent to which this description

---

3. Rippon, 1971. At the news conference following the delivery of this speech, Rippon stated, with some prescience, with regard to the possibility of Guernsey becoming a 'tax haven', that 'There might be a certain amount of envy from within the Community if the islands grow prosperous in this way ... But there is nothing the Common Market countries could do. They have no right under the terms agreed'.

applied. The same concession was extended in respect of persons who had been ordinarily resident in the United Kingdom for five years.

A flurry of legislative activity followed the creation of the Protocol, in particular relating to the Channel Islands' status as part of the customs territory of the Community. *The European Communities (External Tariffs and Non-Discrimination) (Bailiwick of Guernsey) Law, 1972,* brought customs arrangements into line with those of the Community, allowing the States to impose and retain European duties. The Law also repealed legislation requiring aliens to obtain Royal Court consent before buying property. At the accession of the United Kingdom to the Community, workers from other member states were freed from work permit controls. Bailiwick regulations consequently required revision, and on 14 December 1972, the States implemented registration controls under the Immigration Act 1971, which had been extended under The Immigration (Guernsey) Order, 1972. Other enactments amended customs administration and removed certain Commonwealth tariff preferences. Regulation (EEC) No. 706/73, amongst other things, imposed duties and levies, payable to the States, on direct imports from non-Community countries, and confirmed the Bailiwick's historical right of free trade with the United Kingdom. The Regulation also provided that Community rules in areas of trade largely connected with animal husbandry, agriculture, and fisheries products should apply to the islands under the same conditions as they apply to the United Kingdom. *The European Communities (Bailiwick of Guernsey) Law,* 1973 allowed for regulations such as these to have force of law in the Bailiwick, and also dealt with the treatment and proving of Community treaties and instruments before Bailiwick courts, and the collection of customs duties and agricultural levies at Community rates. The Law also made it a criminal offence, punishable in the Bailiwick, to give false evidence on oath before the European Court of Justice (ECJ).

Much of the legislation referred to in the previous paragraph was made by way of Order in Council. Today, laws concerning the Bailiwick's relations with the European Community and Union, and associated regulations and directives applicable under Protocol No. 3, are brought in and applied by Ordinances of the States, as provided for by *The European Communities (Implementation) (Bailiwick of Guernsey) Law,* 1994. European sanctions resolutions are enacted in Guernsey law in the same manner.

As the Community develops, more procedures, regulations, and directives affecting the Common Customs Area and the Common External Tariff extend to the Channel Islands. Some changes to the European Community and Union's constitution, which have had, or are likely to have an effect in the Islands, are described below. However, it remains the case that Protocol No. 3 governs their relations with the European Community. This was explicitly acknowledged in an answer given on 5 June 1989 by the President of the European Commission to written questions from a Member of the European Parliament:

The Channel Islands are not among the countries and territories which are the subject of the special association arrangements set out in Part Four of the EEC Treaty. Moreover, these arrangements apply only to the overseas countries and territories outside Europe.

Pursuant to Article 227(5)(c) of the EEC Treaty, the special arrangements applicable to the Channel Islands come under Protocol No. 3 of the 1972 Act of Accession. This instrument has the same force as the Treaty and could, therefore, be reviewed only through the procedure provided for in Article 236 EEC.

The Commission has no information enabling it to pronounce on the democratic nature of the Channel Islands' institutions.

Under the above Protocol, the Channel Islands are part of the customs territory of the Community. It follows that the Common Customs Tariff, levies and other agricultural import measures apply to trade between the Islands and non-member countries and that there is free movement of goods in trade between the Islands and the Community, as regards both industrial and agricultural products.

However, subject to compliance by the Channel Island authorities with the principle of equal treatment for all natural and legal persons in the Community, the other Community rules do not apply. Implementation of the provisions on the free movement of persons, services and capital is therefore ruled out, as is the case with the provisions of the common policies and, in particular, eligibility for assistance from the structural Funds and under the support measures for agricultural markets [4]

---

4. Quoted in Le Cheminant, 1992 12.

The Maastricht Treaty, 1992

The Treaty on European Union, which was signed at Maastricht on 7 February 1992, and came into force on 1 November 1993, amended the treaties establishing the European Communities, in the most fundamental reform of the European Community since its inception, with the European Coal and Steel Community (ECSC) Treaty, in 1951. It created a 'three pillar' legal structure for the European Union, consisting of an amended European Community Treaty (notably as regards the addition of provisions for economic and monetary union) and two new intergovernmental sections covering co-operation in foreign and security policy, and police and judicial co-operation in criminal matters. Certain of the Maastricht Treaty's titles and protocols were brought into Bailiwick law, within the terms of the 1972 Treaty and Protocol No. 3, by *The European Communities (Amendment) (Bailiwick of Guernsey) Ordinance*, 1994.

Following meetings held between representatives of the Channel Islands and the Isle of Man with United Kingdom Government officials, the Home Office clarified the Treaty's implications for the Islands, in a letter to be found in a *Billet d'État* considered by the States of Guernsey on 27 July 1994. The Home Office drew attention to Title VI, which concerns justice and home affairs, stating that:

> It would be for the Islands themselves to decide whether, and to what extent, they wished to be included in measures negotiated under the Chapter. The United Kingdom undertakes that the Islands will be fully consulted about measures which may affect them and which are to be negotiated under Title VI. No such measure will be applied to any of the Islands without the consent of the authorities for the Island in question.

This 'opt in' arrangement has led to Guernsey's authorities voluntarily participating in criminal and civil justice initiatives. The progressive economic integration of Community markets, particularly as a result of the Single Market initiative in 1985, and the drive to economic and monetary union, has to an extent affected the degree of competition to which the Bailiwick's financial sectors, and trade and industry, are exposed.[5]

---

5. Le Cheminant, 1992 3.

The Maastricht Treaty's provisions concerning Union citizenship, taken with Article 4 of Protocol No. 3, suggest that the islands' authorities may not discriminate on the grounds of nationality against European citizens, although the precise scope of Article 4 remains unclear despite two ECJ rulings.[6] Even with the benefit of these two rulings, it is still not clear whether, directly or indirectly, the provisions on citizenship introduced by the Maastricht Treaty (including the right of Union citizens to diplomatic protection by all Member States and the right to petition or apply to the European Parliament and the Ombudsman) extend to, or can be invoked by, Channel Islanders. As the Home Office letter published in 1994 set out, this and certain other provisions of the Treaty have yet to be tested in law.

The European Economic Area Agreement, 1992

The Agreement on the European Economic Area (EEA) was signed on 2 May 1992, and adjusted by protocol on 17 March 1993. The Agreement provides for the participation of Norway, Iceland, and Liechtenstein in the Single European Market, which had been envisaged in the Single European Act of 1986. It principally relates to the free movement of goods, persons, services, and capital, and contains further provisions essentially applying EC rules on competition and state aid, social policy, consumer protection, the environment, statistics, and company law to the EEA. The Agreement was brought into Bailiwick law, subject to the terms of the Treaty of 1972 and Protocol No. 3, by *The European Communities (Amendment) (Bailiwick of Guernsey) Ordinance,* 1994. The effect of the EEA Agreement on the Bailiwick is to extend the Community's rules on the free movement of goods, which apply to the Bailiwick by virtue of Article 1 of Protocol No. 3, to trade with Norway,

---

6. In *Department of Health and Social Security v Barr and Montrose Holdings Limited,* a case referred to the ECJ from the Isle of Man in 1989, and in *Roque v the Lieutenant Governor of Jersey,* referred to the ECJ by the Royal Court of Jersey in 1996, the ECJ held that areas of Community law other than those expressly covered by Protocol No. 3 were not applicable in the Protocol No. 3 territories, although, in the words of the Judgment of the Court of 16 July 1998 (*European Court reports* 1998 I-04607) 'the prohibition of any discrimination between natural and legal persons from the Member States in relation to situations which, in territories where the Treaty is fully applicable, are governed by Community law', is applicable there by virtue of Article 4 of that Protocol.

Iceland and Liechtenstein. In substantive terms, the EEA Agreement has no effect on the extent to which Community law applies to the Bailiwick under Protocol No. 3.

The Treaty of Amsterdam, 1997

The Treaty of Amsterdam, which amended and supplemented the existing Treaties, was signed on 2 October 1997, and entered into force on 1 May 1999. The Treaty amended both the Treaty on European Union, and the European Community Treaty. The former was supplemented by new provisions on a common foreign and security policy, on police and judicial co-operation in criminal matters, and on 'closer co-operation'. The EC Treaty was developed by the addition of new provisions, amongst others, relating to visa, asylum, the free movement of persons, employment, social policy, health, and environmental protection. The Amsterdam Treaty, like the Maastricht Treaty before it and the Nice Treaty since, extended the legislative and 'watchdog' functions of the European Parliament, and also the number of areas in which the Council could adopt legislation by qualified majority voting. As with the Maastricht Treaty, by their own Ordinances the States of Guernsey may 'opt in' to certain arrangements and legislation brought about in consequence of the Amsterdam Treaty.

The European Court of Justice

Unlike the European Court of Human Rights (treated in Chapter four), which is an institution of the Council of Europe, the ECJ is an institution of the European Union. It sits in Luxembourg, and was created in 1952 as one of the institutions of the ECSC. It interprets and applies Community law, and its jurisdiction covers, in broad terms, actions for judicial review brought by natural or legal persons, Member States, or the Community institutions, against one or other institution, and also actions where national courts or tribunals may refer questions on the validity or interpretation of Community law to the ECJ for preliminary rulings. The application of Community law in the Channel Islands by virtue of Protocol No. 3 is therefore subject to the ECJ's jurisdiction.

The Court of First Instance

Since 1989, the ECJ has been complemented by a Court of First Instance (CFI). The CFI was conceived to alleviate the workload of the ECJ, notably in cases involving the assessment of detailed economic matters, as well as in 'administrative' or staff cases arising out of disputes between EC civil servants and the institutions. The workload of the CFI now comprises all actions brought by private parties and tends to be dominated by competition, state aid, customs and trade matters. Currently, cases brought by Member States or the institutions must originate in the ECJ, which also has the exclusive jurisdiction to hear cases referred by national courts and tribunals. The ECJ also hears appeals on points of law from the CFI. On matters falling within the scope of Protocol No. 3, the Court of First Instance, like the ECJ, might adjudicate in Channel Island matters if called upon to do so.

European Monetary Union

The Bailiwick of Guernsey has its own currency, which is expressed in the same denominations as British Sterling. The latter circulates freely. Since 1921, parity has been maintained between the two currencies.[7] The Maastricht Treaty introduced provisions establishing a legal framework for European Monetary Union (EMU). This envisioned the use of a common European currency, known from 1995 as the *Euro,* and the establishment of a European Central Bank. In May 1997, the States' Advisory and Finance Committee formed a working party to study the likely consequences of EMU for Guernsey. The working party noted that Guernsey's economy is too small to support its own stable currency, and therefore it has to be linked to the currency of another jurisdiction. In 2002, Austria, Belgium, Finland, France, Germany, Greece, Ireland, Italy, Luxembourg, the Netherlands, Portugal, and Spain adopted the Euro as their sole currency. The United Kingdom may follow. Whilst it is theoretically possible to link Guernsey's currency to one other than that of the United Kingdom, for example the Swiss Franc or United States' Dollar, it appears inevitable that if the United Kingdom (the islands' main trading partner) adopts the Euro, the Bailiwick will do so as well. Since Protocol No. 3 exclusively defines the current relationship

---

7. McCammon, 1984 185–86.

of the Channel Islands and the Isle of Man with the European Community, the islands cannot join the EMU as such without an amendment to the Protocol, which would have to be negotiated and agreed by all EU Member States and ratified by their parliaments.

The situation concerning EMU exemplifies an aspect of the Bailiwick's developing relations with the European Community and Union. Whilst some European laws, agreements and other arrangements are introduced in the islands pursuant to their status under Protocol No. 3, and the Treaty of 1972, increasingly other regulations are made and relations entered into at the island's election, for commercial reasons, or in the interests of maintaining international political relations, or developing island law. Even if, in formal terms, the relationship of the Islands with the EC or EU remains that set out in Protocol No. 3 (as interpreted by the ECJ) the network of ties between the Channel Islands and Europe is far more intricate and substantial than the system of largely commercial relations of the nineteen-seventies.

Postscript: the European Constitution – continuity and change

Following a European Council meeting held on 17 and 18 June 2004, a provisional text of The New Treaty Establishing a Constitution for Europe was published, and was signed by the Heads of State and Government of the twenty-five Member States of the EU and the three candidate countries on 29 October 2004. Its main intentions are to simplify and codify the existing EU framework and its procedures by the uniting of all present treaties in a single document, abolishing the 'three pillar' structure, amending the Council presidency system and creating a position of EU foreign minister, and limiting the veto powers of Member States. Some limited revision of EU functions in the areas of justice and home affairs, and foreign, security and defence policies is also intended, and a simplification of procedures fostering greater transparency and democracy is envisaged.

All twenty-five Member States will have to complete the ratification process before the Constitutional Treaty comes into force. In some States this will be dependent upon the outcome of referenda, and even if all Members elect in favour of ratification, it is not anticipated that the Constitutional Treaty will come into force before 2006. As part of the ratification process and according to convention, the United Kingdom Government has consulted and will continue to consult Guernsey's authorities. The consolidating effect of the Constitutional Treaty means that the Treaty of Accession of the United Kingdom to the European Community of 1972 and with it Protocol No. 3 on the Channel Islands and the Isle of Man will be superseded. A new protocol to the new Constitutional Treaty, which will preserve the position of the Bailiwick of Guernsey enshrined in Protocol No. 3 has however been drafted, and at a meeting of the States of Deliberation held on 25 February 2004, the Chief Minister was able to announce that, following a series of interventions by the Crown Dependencies to ensure that the scope and effect of Protocol No. 3 was not altered, the United Kingdom Government and the technical group of legal advisors working on the draft Treaty had accepted the islands' proposals, and that it was confidently expected that these would similarly be acceptable to the intergovernmental conference which had been launched in October 2003. Neither at the intergovernmental conference, nor at the European Council meeting which followed on 17 and 18 June 2004, was any suggestion made that this confidence was misplaced. The new protocol is worded in practically the same terms as Protocol no. 3 of 1972, although with minor amendments to reflect the fact that the transitional provisions no longer apply, and there has also been some updating of terminology. The new protocol appears as Articles 8 to 13 of Protocol 8 to the new Constitutional Treaty, being Section 3 of Title II of that Protocol. If the Constitutional Treaty is found to be acceptable to all Member States and duly comes into force it therefore appears that the formal constitutional relationship of the Bailiwick of Guernsey to the European Union will remain the same as that created under Protocol No. 3, and the Treaty of 1972.

11. Guernsey and the World

Guernsey may have expressed a degree of autonomy internationally as early as the fifteenth century. In 1481, an assembly (possibly the States themselves, in an early form) met to appoint attorneys to complete certain *obligations* entered into with the Admiral of France.[1] Perhaps these related to the Papal Bull of neutrality of that year. This exceptional reference apart, responsibility for the island's international relations clearly fell within the Royal prerogative, and it was customary from the thirteenth century for the Crown to pay Guernsey close attention, especially in consideration of its proximity to an often hostile Continent.

Her Majesty's Government remains generally responsible for the defence and international relations of the Bailiwick. Some arrangements entered into by United Kingdom governments on the Bailiwick of Guernsey's behalf are detailed below. Other international agreements include European regulations and directives made in the context of Protocol No. 3 of the Treaty of Accession of the United Kingdom to Europe, now brought into Bailiwick law by Ordinance.

Letters and memoranda published in a *Billet d'État* for 25 February 1970, which supply the material presented in this and the next paragraph, described the somewhat complicated position of the Channel Islands in relation to treaties and international agreements at that date. Before 1950, the United Kingdom authorities regarded such instruments as extending to the Islands unless the contrary was expressly provided. The Home Office, whilst always seeking island observations on agreements that might apply to them, very often found the consultation period too short and otherwise impractical. In that year, therefore, the Government concluded that it would be better if international agreements and treaties did not extend to the Islands unless these were particularly named, and that thenceforth the Channel Islands should usually be regarded as among the territories for whose international relations the Government was responsible. A Home Office letter to the

---

1. De Guérin, 1914 163–4.

Lieutenant-Governor of 8 March 1951, conveying a Foreign Office circular of 16 October 1950 setting this out, stated that in '... such a case it will be open to the Insular Authorities to accede to an agreement if after examination of its provisions at their leisure they should at any time desire to do so'.

Difficulties arose, however, and a further Home Office letter, of 30 December 1966, confusingly asserted that the effect of the decision transmitted by its earlier letter was to make it possible for the United Kingdom Government to include the Channel Islands in international agreements containing an article allowing states to extend the application of agreements to dependent territories 'at a convenient time, after the United Kingdom had become a party'. The letter concluded

> The position then is that the United Kingdom's acceptance of agreements containing no indication of limited territorial application binds all the United Kingdom's dependent territories including the Channel Islands and the Isle of Man. Before concluding such agreements, however, Her Majesty's Government will always endeavour to discuss the implications as fully as possible with the Insular Authorities.

The necessity of consultations taking place was stressed in the Report of the Royal Commission on the Constitution, 1969–73, which pointed to situations where the application of agreements requires the creation of legislation of a sort properly the province of the Island legislatures.[2]

A Home Office memorandum dated 3 February 1993 ironed out the ambiguities between the United Kingdom's statements of 1950 and 1966, establishing the position with regard to the application of treaties to the Crown Dependencies, reviewing international law, and United Kingdom departmental and international practices.[3] Effectively, since 1967, when completing instruments of ratification and accession, United Kingdom Governments have expressed the territorial extent of commitments entered into. Whitehall Departments today consult Guernsey's authorities at an early stage before completing a treaty or agreement, in order to ascertain whether the island wishes the arrangement to apply to it, and if so to consider any textual modifications that might be required: in the

---

2. Commission 1969–73, 1973 para. 1363.
3. Cf. Commission 1969–73, 1973 paras 1381–88.

words of a report presented by the United Kingdom Government to the 2000 Ministerial on the implementation of the Organisation for Economic Co-operation and Development anti-bribery convention, in a manner that set out actual modern practice, 'the ratification of international conventions and treaties may be extended to them [*the Crown Dependencies and the U.K. Overseas Territories*], subject to the agreement of the Insular Authorities'.[4]

The United Kingdom Government will separately specify the territorial extent of the application of treaties entered into under the auspices of the United Nations and other global organisations at the time of signature, ratification, or accession. In arrangements entered into under the auspices of other organisations, for example the Council of Europe, an article will usually refer to the territorial application of the agreement within the text itself. The United Kingdom Treaty of Accession to Europe of 1972 and the special position of the Channel Islands under it governs relations with the European Union, as seen above. Again, in these instances, the United Kingdom Government will seek the views of the island authorities on all such agreements, and the application and extension of them to their jurisdictions.

The United Nations

The United Nations Act 1946 was registered in Guernsey on 7 February 1967. Resolutions of the Security Council made under the United Nations Charter can be implemented in United Kingdom domestic law by Orders in Council, which can be made so as to extend to any part of the Dominions, an expression that includes the Channel Islands. Such Orders in Council are agreed by the island authorities and registered by the Royal Court. The United Nations International Covenant on Civil and Political Rights (1966) and the United Nations International Covenant on Economic, Social and Cultural Rights (also of 1966) were both ratified by the United Kingdom on 20 August 1976. These also extend to the Bailiwick. (The Optional Protocol of the International Covenant on Civil and Political Rights, in contrast, has not been ratified, and neither United Kingdom nor Bailiwick citizens have a personal right to petition the Human Rights

---

4. 'United Kingdom review of implementation of the convention and 1997 recommendation' (http://www.oecd.org/dataoecd/8/24/2754266.pdf), accessed 2 April 2004.

Committee set up to receive and consider communications from individuals asserting violations of Covenant rights). In connection with these instruments, the States periodically report to the United Nations on the implementation of covenant rights, with civil servants and Law Officers attending to answer questions as necessary.

The Organisation for Economic Co-operation and Development

The Organisation for Economic Co-operation and Development (OECD) replaced the post-war Organisation for European Economic Co-operation, which had administered the Marshall Plan. The OECD promotes policies that aim to achieve high and sustainable economic development in member countries, maintaining financial stability, whilst at the same time raising standards of living. It also seeks to advance global economic development and foster the expansion of trade. Its concerns with democracy and economics have resulted in monitoring activities and the preparation of surveys and international agreements progressing its aims.

The convention founding the OECD was completed in Paris on 14 December 1960. The United Kingdom was one of twenty original signatories. At ratification, on 2 May 1961, the United Kingdom failed to specify the territorial application of the Convention, and doubts arose as to its extent. Therefore, by a letter of 20 July 1990, the British Ambassador in Paris confirmed to the Government of France, the depository state of the OECD Convention, that the Convention applied to the Channel Islands, the Isle of Man, Gibraltar, and Bermuda. A letter dated the day before, addressed by the head of the United Kingdom OECD Delegation to its Secretary General, confirmed that future recommendations, decisions (binding and otherwise) and agreements, as provided for by Article Five of the Convention, would extend to those territories, unless the contrary was indicated, and, further, that past decisions and recommendations applied to the same extent as they did in the United Kingdom. By *The Organisation for Economic Co-operation and Development (Guernsey and Alderney) Law*, 1994, and *The Organisation for Economic Co-operation and Development (Sark) Law*, 1994, the capacities and status of the OECD were recognised in Bailiwick law, and the Organisation and its officers, members' representatives, organs, and experts performing missions for it were afforded privileges, immunities, exemptions, and reliefs similar to those accorded them by member states.

In 1998 the OECD published a report called *Harmful Tax Competition: an emerging global issue*. This, and later reports and statements, identified certain practices in geographically mobile services, including the financial sector, and recommended measures to counteract them. In June 2000, the OECD listed thirty-five jurisdictions that met the Organisation's technical criteria, identifying them as 'tax havens'. Guernsey and Jersey were amongst these. Building upon Guernsey's existing record in financial regulation and the exchange of information in criminal tax matters, a letter of 21 February 2002 from the President of the States' Advisory and Finance Committee to the Secretary-General of the OECD made a general political commitment to the improvement of transparency in tax systems, and the establishment by the island of tax information exchange agreements with other jurisdictions. The letter went on to refer, not unreasonably, to the island's expectation that the OECD would not require Guernsey to make greater commitments, nor satisfy more onerous standards, than those required of other jurisdictions, including member states themselves (such, although the letter did not name them, as Luxembourg and Switzerland, which had not been identified by the OECD as 'tax havens'), stressing that the island regarded as essential to its participation in the initiative ' ... the establishment of a level playing field among all OECD member countries and also those non-member jurisdictions with which it is materially in competition in the provision of cross-border financial services ... '.[5]

Tax Information Exchange Agreements

In a ceremony held in Washington D.C. on 19 September 2002, acting pursuant to the agreement with the OECD that is the subject of the previous paragraph, Guernsey completed a tax information exchange agreement with the United States. The agreement formalised existing co-operation in criminal tax affairs, and in civil tax matters enabled the exchange of information. It was signed by the United States' Treasury Secretary and the President of the States of Guernsey's Advisory and Finance Committee, as its nominee and after the Committee had received advice from the Administrator of Income Tax and the Law Officers, as authorised by a States' resolution of 10 July 2002.

---

5. Rowland, 2002 ii recounts this episode and reflects upon it in context.

Guernsey is continuing to discuss the terms of possible bilateral tax information exchange agreements with a number of countries (at present discussions are taking place with Australia, New Zealand, France, Germany, the Netherlands, and Ireland) though completion of these once terms have been finalised will depend on the 'level playing field' issue.

The Commonwealth

Guernsey is not an independent Commonwealth member, but does participate in some of its institutions, and may in the future enjoy associate status. The Law Officers of the Crown are regularly represented at meetings of the Ministers of Law and Attorneys General of Small Commonwealth Jurisdictions, and recently Her Majesty's Procureur for the first time attended the full Law Ministers Conference, as part of the United Kingdom delegation. The last President of the Advisory and Finance Committee was one of a similar delegation attending the annual meeting of Commonwealth finance ministers. The States are full members of the Commonwealth Parliamentary Association, actively participating in the Association's regional meetings, and a Guernsey team takes part in the Commonwealth Games. The Royal Commonwealth Society has a Guernsey branch, and indeed the Bailiff and Lieutenant-Governor are *ex officio* vice-presidents of the parent body.

The British-Irish Council

The British-Irish Agreement of 2 December 1999, which implemented the Belfast or Good Friday Agreement of the previous year, amongst other things created the British-Irish Council. Its purpose is to promote harmony between members and mutual benefit for their peoples, through co-operation on matters of common interest. The British and Irish governments, together with those of Guernsey, Jersey, and the Isle of Man, and the devolved institutions of Scotland, Wales, and Northern Ireland are represented. The President of the former States' Advisory and Finance Committee (now the island's Chief Minister) and the Chief Executive of the States of Guernsey have so far represented Guernsey at Council summits, which normally are held twice a year. Priority areas of mutual concern so far identified by the Council are drugs, the environment, the knowledge economy, social inclusion, tourism, transport, telemedicine, and indigenous languages. Each member has been designated a 'lead administration' in respect of one or more of these areas, with Guernsey presently having responsibility for tourism. Future areas of concern to the Council are likely to include agriculture, sport, energy, education, and European issues. The Council provides an international forum where matters such as these can be discussed and common policies agreed. The Good Friday Agreement also referred to facilitating co-operation and dialogue between the Parliaments of Ireland and Britain, and membership of the British-Irish Inter-Parliamentary body created in 1990 was in 2001 expanded to include membership of all administrations represented on the British-Irish Council.

An international personality

Although Her Majesty's Government retains its long-standing responsibility for some aspects of Guernsey's international relations, in other respects the island has expressed a distinct personality. For example, *The Maintenance Orders (Facilities for Enforcement) (Guernsey) Law*, 1955 and *The Judgments (Reciprocal Enforcement) (Guernsey) Law*, 1957 provide for the registration and enforcement in Guernsey of orders made and judgments given in reciprocating states that offer the like arrangement in respect of orders and judgments of Guernsey's Royal Court.

In recent years, developments have been most noticeable in respect of international financial regulation. Guernsey was represented by its own officials in the negotiations with the OECD, leading to the arrangement recorded by the letter of 21 February 2002. This letter was issued by the Advisory and Finance Committee, a Committee of the States of Guernsey, and not the United Kingdom Government on their behalf. Similarly, island representatives worked directly with officials of the United States Treasury over the tax information exchange agreement of 2002, and continue to do so with other jurisdictions. In connection with these negotiations, the United Kingdom government has provided a 'letter of entrustment' – as originally required to satisfy the government of the United States – confirming the island's right, within the area of domestic competence, to negotiate and conclude such agreements with other territories, and that the obligations contained in such agreements are those of the parties alone.

With regard to Guernsey's negotiations with the European Union over the latter's Savings Tax Directive, the island has agreed to ensure that its banks will hold back on behalf of foreign jurisdictions certain taxes owed outside the island, and this will require the introduction of domestic legislation, enforcement by the island's authorities, and the completion of further agreements exclusively between Guernsey and sovereign territories.

The invitation to the Crown Dependencies to participate in the British-Irish Council is also symptomatic of a development in their status, offering the opportunity for direct communication between them and a distinct sovereign power, namely the Republic of Ireland. Greater independence also appears to be developing in the island's participation in the work of the Commonwealth.

In part, it is the growth of island capabilities that has contributed to Guernsey's government taking a more independent role in international affairs, but there are also other causes that might account for the changes, including an increased recognition of variations in island and United Kingdom interests, a developing culture of decentralisation in the United Kingdom, and changes in European and domestic law, subjecting the activity of the United Kingdom government to greater judicial scrutiny.

The question of independence

In recent years, calls for independence have followed perceived slights to Guernsey's constitutional status. These suggestions, by individuals, have met with no popular enthusiasm, in fact little obvious reaction at all. At the time of the United Kingdom's bids to join the European Community, Roy Jenkins and others did suggest that, in the circumstances of the time, the Channel Islands might wish to become independent. Theoretically, this would appear to be possible. The United Nations' Declaration on the Granting of Independence to Colonial Countries and Peoples, adopted by General Assembly resolution 1514 (xv) of 14 December 1960, avows that all peoples have a right to self-determination. This was reiterated in Article 1 of The United Nations International Covenant on Civil and Political Rights, of 1966, which reads 'All peoples have the right of self-determination. By virtue of that right they freely determine their political status and freely pursue their economic, social and cultural development'. Whilst the Declaration and Covenant were hardly made with the Crown Dependencies in mind, there appears to be no reason to doubt that the islands' populations might not seek full political independence, following the precedents of former trust and non-self-governing territories of the United Kingdom. Established procedures suggest a referendum – now provided for in island law, as noted in Chapter four – in favour of independence followed by a constitutional conference would be necessary.

Merely because a thing is possible, does not mean that it is desirable. It is not easy to imagine, in terms of international relations, that Guernsey would fare very well without the continued maintenance of the Crown's obligations towards the island. In the international arena, Guernsey's government is often able at present to have a voice. Institutions have developed in such a way that the island's authorities may communicate with United Kingdom negotiators and representatives working with international organisations, and agreement is sought before the extension of international conventions and treaties. The internal stability and good relations with the United Kingdom enjoyed by the island's financial institutions probably would be lost, or modified detrimentally, if the island sought full statehood, and monies currently attracted from the City of London and other places might well flow elsewhere. Equally the amount of business flowing from Guernsey to London might be diminished. Taking on its own responsibilities for defence, diplomatic representation, and the management of air navigation, to name some examples, would place considerable strains on Guernsey's administrative and economic structures. Independence would not, at least in the present circumstances, appear to be an attractive proposition. Guernsey's relations – commercial, institutional, and constitutional – with the United Kingdom appear on the whole to work to mutual advantage, in the mature situation described above.

At the same time, differences in the United Kingdom's and Guernsey's policies, interests, and obligations do occur, and the governments of each will quite properly seek to meet their respective responsibilities and undertakings. The existing and developing international personality referred to above suggests a way forward. As long as the United Kingdom government does its best to ensure that the island enjoys 'a level playing field' internationally, to quote the letter to the OECD of 21 February 2002, including to the extent of facilitating and encouraging direct relations between the government of Guernsey and third parties, this provides for the continuance of the island's evolved, and evolving, government and legal systems. Guernsey's best response to developing issues is to continue to assert the essence of its constitution: the ancient and fundamental right of its citizens to their own law and institutions.

Bibliography

Anon. (1837–38) 'Defence of the Chartered Rights and Privileges of Guernsey', *The Guernsey and Jersey Magazine* 4, 368–79; 5, 49–52, 101–10, 161–68

Ashley, A. (1953) 'Property in Relation to Marriage and the Family: iii the Channel Islands, with a final note of comparison with Scotland', *The Juridical Review* 65, 262–93

Aubin, C. (1984) 'La tenure par bordage en Normandie tant continentale qu'insulaire', Mémoire de Maîtrise, Université de Caen, Histoire

Axton, M. and Axton, R. (1991) *Calendar and Catalogue of Sark Seigneurie Archive 1526–1927*, Kew

Bailhache, W. (2001) 'The Constitutional Relationship between Jersey and the UK', *Association of Contentious Trust and Probate Specialists Newsletter* 28–29 (Sept.), 5–10

Bailhache, W. (2002) The text of a statement made in the States of Jersey on 15 May 2002 under the headline: 'Tax: Parliament has no power to legislate for Jersey against its will', *Jersey Evening Post* 16 May, 16

Baker, J. (1990) *An Introduction to English Legal History*, London

Barber, P. (1995) 'What is a Peculiar?', *Ecclesiastical Law Journal* 16, 299–312

Beaumont, J. (1993) *The Constitution and Administration of Sark*, Guernsey

Bell, W. (2002) *Guernsey: occupied but never conquered*, Exeter

Beloff, M. (2003) 'A legal step that had to be taken', *The Observer*, 15 June

Besnier, R. (1935) *La Coutume de Normandie: histoire externe*, Paris

Blackstone, W. (1825) *Commentaries on the Laws of England*, (1765–9), 4 vols, sixteenth edition, London

Bois, F. (1972) *A Constitutional History of Jersey*, Jersey

Bromley, J. (1986) 'A New Vocation: privateering and the wars of 1689–97 and 1702–13' in Jamieson, A. (ed.), *A People of the Sea: the maritime history of the Channel Islands*, London, 109–47

Carey, de V. (1991) 'The Clameur de Haro', *Guernsey Law Journal* 11, 31–35

Carey, E. (ed.) (1925) *Actes des États de l'Île de Guernesey*, vol. 4 1815–22, Guernsey

Carey, L. (1889) *Essai sur les Institutions, Lois et Coûtumes de l'Île de Guernesey*, (*c.* 1769), Guernsey

Carré, H. (1843) *De la Constitution de l'Isle de Guernesey et de sa Réforme; ou recherches sur la nature de ses principes, et sur leur application pratique*, Guernsey

Cartel, A. (1994) *Lower Normandy and the Channel Islands/La Basse-Normandie et les îles anglo-normandes* (Basse-Normandie Report, Conseil Economique et Social Régional), n.p.

Chaplais, P. (1957) 'The Chancery of Guyenne 1289–1453', in J. Conway Davies (ed.), *Studies presented to Sir Hilary Jenkinson*, London, 61–96

Clark, R. (1984) 'Mr Warburton's Treatise on the History, Laws and Customs of Guernsey', *Transactions of La Société Guernesiaise* 21, 547–51

Coates, R. (1991) *The Ancient and Modern Names of the Channel Islands*, Stamford

Coke, E. (1817) *The Fourth Part of the Institutes of the Laws of England; concerning the jurisdiction of the Courts*, (first printed 1644), London

Commission 1579 (1579) Documents of the Royal Commission appointed 27 July 1579, National Archives, Kew: C47/10/12

Commission 1607 (1814) *Reglemens des Commissaires Royaux, envoyés par S.M. le Roi Jacques I. L'Année 1607*, Guernsey

Commission 1815 (1823) *Changes erected in the Laws of Guernsey in 1823, to which are prefixed the Report of the Royal Commissioners deputed to that island in 1815; the observations of the Royal Court, and the answers of the Right Honourable the Lords of His Majesty's Most Honourable Privy Council*, Guernsey

Commission 1846 (1848) *Second Report of the Commissioners appointed to inquire into the state of the criminal law in the Channel Islands – Guernsey*, London

Commission 1969–73 (1973) *Royal Commission on the Constitution 1969–1973: volume 1 Report*, London

Corbeau, H. (1934) *La situation juridique des Iles Anglo-Normandes dans l'Empire Britannique*, Caen

Cornes, R. (2000) '*McGonnell v UK*, the Lord Chancellor and the Law Lords' *Public Law* 166–177

Crook, D. (1982) *Records of the General Eyre*, London

Cross, F. and Livingstone, E. (1997) *The Oxford Dictionary of the Christian Church*, third edition, Oxford

Cruickshank, C. (1975) *The German Occupation of the Channel Islands*, London

Cunliffe, B. (1986) 'The First Eight Thousand Years, 7000 BC – AD 1000', in Jamieson, A. (ed.), *A People of the Sea: the maritime history of the Channel Islands*, London, 1–18

Curtis, S. (1939) 'The Seals of the Royal Court of Guernsey', *Transactions of La Société Guernesiaise* 13, 255–60

Dasent, J. (ed.) (1893) *Acts of the Privy Council of England* new series vol. 7 1558–70, London

Dasent, J. (ed.) (1895) *Acts of the Privy Council of England* new series vol. 11 1578–80, London

Dasent, J. (ed.) (1900) *Acts of the Privy Council of England* new series vol. 21 1591, London

Dawes, G. (2003) *Laws of Guernsey*, Oxford

de Cléry, R. (1898) *Les Iles Normandes: pays de Home Rule*, second edition, Paris

de Ferrière, C-J (1762) *Dictionnaire de Droit et de Pratique*, 2 vols, Paris

de Gruchy, G. (1922) 'The Entries relating to Jersey in the Great Rolls of the Exchequer of Normandy of A.D. 1180', Société Jersiaise *Bulletin Annuel* 9, 18–44

de Gruchy, G. (1957) *Medieval Land Tenures in Jersey*, Jersey

de Gruchy, W. (ed.) (1881) *L'Ancienne Coutume de Normandie: réimpression éditée avec légères annotations*, Jersey

de Guérin, T. (1909) i 'Feudalism in Guernsey', *Transactions of La Société Guernesiaise* 6, 58–82

de Guérin, T. (1909) ii 'Some important events in Guernsey history', *Transactions of La Société Guernesiaise* 6, 99–121

de Guérin, T. (1914) 'Notes on some old documents', *Transactions of La Société Guernesiaise* 7, 151–68

de Guérin, T. (1919) 'Notes on the early constitutional history of the Channel Islands', *Transactions of La Société Guernesiaise* 8, 174–87

de H(avilland), T. (1847) *Some Remarks on the Constitution of Guernsey, one of the Channel Islands, formerly a part of the Duchy of Normandy*, Guernsey

de Sausmarez, C. (1965) 'The story of William Le Marchant, Bailiff of Guernsey, 1770–1800: a lost page of Guernsey history', *Transactions of La Société Guernesiaise* 17, 717–46

de Sausmarez, H. (1928) 'The earlier charters of Guernsey: with particular reference to those of 15 Edward III, and 1 Henry VII', *Transactions of La Société Guernesiaise* 10, 250–59

de Sausmarez, H. (1930) *Guernsey and the Imperial Contribution*, Guernsey

de Sausmarez, H. (ed.) (1934) *The Extentes of Guernsey 1248 and 1331 and other documents relating to ancient usages and customs in that island*, Guernsey

de Smith, S, and Brazier, R. (1998) *Constitutional and Administrative Law*, eighth edition, London

Devyck, L. (1583) 'Coustumes et Usages de l'Isle de Guernesay', British Library, Department of Manuscripts, Sloane MS 2446

Dicey, A. (1915) *Introduction to the Study of the Law of the Constitution*, eighth edition, London, repr. Indianapolis 1982

Duncan, J. (1841) *The History of Guernsey; with occasional notices of Jersey, Alderney, and Sark, and biographical sketches*, London

Eagleston, A. (1924) 'Parliamentary analogies from the Channel Islands', *History* 9, 103–109

Eagleston, A. (1949) *The Channel Islands under Tudor Government 1485–1642: a study in administrative history*, Cambridge

Edwards, A. (1998) *Review of Financial Regulations in the Crown Dependencies*, 4 parts, London (Cm 4109)

Elton, G. (ed.) (1982) *The Tudor Constitution: documents and commentary*, second edition, Cambridge

Everard, J., and Holt, J. (2004) *Jersey 1204: the forging of an island community*, London

Ewen, A. (1961) 'The Fiefs of the Island of Guernsey', *Transactions of La Société Guernesiaise* 17, 173–209

Ewen, A., and de Carteret, A. (1969) *The Fief of Sark*, Guernsey

Fauroux, M. (ed.) (1961) *Recueil des Actes des Ducs de Normandie (911–1066)*, Caen

Finnis, J. (1991–2001) 'The Channel Islands and the Isle of Man', *Halsbury's Laws of England*, fourth edition reissue, 56 vols, London, with cumulative supplement (ed. Q. Hailsham *et al.*), vol. 6, 381–87

Gahan, F. (1963) 'Criminal Law in Guernsey', *Solicitor Quarterly* 2, 148–60

Gillett, J. (1990) *The Juvenile Court of Guernsey*, Guernsey

Haldane, R. (2001) 'Jersey Prison Board Case: notes of proposed arguments' (1894), *The Jersey Law Review* 5, 254–70

Hansard (2000) HL Official Report, May 3

Harwood, P. *et al.* (2000) *Report of the Panel to Review the Machinery of Government in Guernsey*, Guernsey

Harwood, P. *et al.* (2001) *Statement of Views of the Panel to Review the Machinery of Government in Guernsey*, Guernsey

Havet, J. (1878) *Les Cours Royales des Iles Normandes*, Paris

Havet, J. (1896) *Oeuvres de Julien Havet*, 2 vols, Paris

Heylyn, P. (1656) *A Full Relation of two Journeys: The One Into the Main–Land of France, the Other Into some of the adjacent Ilands* (from p. 277: *The Second Journey: containing a survey of the estate of the two Ilands Guernzey and Jarsey, with the Isles appending. According to their Politie, and Formes of Government, both* Ecclesiasticall *and* Civill), (1629), London

Heyting, W. (1977) *The Constitutional Relationship between Jersey and the United Kingdom*, Jersey

Hibbs, L. (1998) 'Jersey Canon Law – its "peculiar" status', Société Jersiaise *Bulletin Annuel* 27, 257–62

Hocart, R. (1988) *An Island Assembly: the development of the States of Guernsey 1700–1949*, Guernsey

Holt, J. (1975) 'The End of the Anglo-Norman Realm' (Raleigh Lecture on History, 1975), *Proceedings of the British Academy* 61, 223–65

Horner, S. (1984) *The Isle of Man and the Channel Islands: a study of their status under constitutional, international and European law* (European University Institute working paper no. 98), Badia Fiesolana

Hoüard, D. (1780–82) *Dictionnaire Analytique, Historique, Étymologique, Critique et Interprétatif de la Coutume de Normandie*, 4 vols, Rouen

Howell, P. (1979) *The Judicial Committee of the Privy Council 1833–1876*, Cambridge

Jacob, J. (1830) *Annals of some of the British Norman Isles constituting the Bailiwick of Guernsey*, part i, Paris

Jacqueline, B. (1978) 'Sixte IV et la Piraterie dans les Iles Anglo-Normandes (1480)', *Revue du Département de la Manche* 20, 197–202

Jehan, T. (1983) 'Summary of Parochial Administration', typescript at St Peter Port Constables' Office

Jeremie, P. (1861) Evidence given in 1860 by Advocate Peter Jeremie, of Guernsey, contained in the *Report of the Commissioners appointed to inquire into the civil, municipal, and ecclesiastical laws of the island of Jersey*, London, 671–98

Jeremie, P. (1866) *On the Law of Real Property in Guernsey*, Guernsey

Jowell, J. (2001) 'The Scope of Guernsey's Autonomy: a brief rejoinder', *The Jersey Law Review* 5, 271–77

Lawrence, A. (1926) 'Appendix' to Report No. 563 of the Convocation of Canterbury *Report of the Joint Committee on the representation of the Channel Islands*

Le Cerf, T. (1863) *L'Archipel des Iles Normandes: Jersey, Guernesey, Auregny, Sark et dépendances. Institutions communales, judiciaires, féodales de ces Iles*, Paris

Le Cheminant, F. *et al* (1991) *Guernsey, The European Community and 1992*, Guernsey

Le Cras, A. (1839) *The Laws, Customs, and Privileges, and their administration, in the island of Jersey; with notices of Guernsey; also a commentary on certain abuses, and a petition to Parliament for a reform of the same*, London

Lee, G. (ed.) (1889) 'Extraits des Registres du Secrètariat de l'Évêché de Coutances 1487–1557', Société Jersiaise *Bulletin Annuel* 2, 404–60

Lee, G. (ed.) (1904) 'Documents concerning the transfer of the Ecclesiastical Jurisdiction over the Channel Islands from the See of Coutances to those of Salisbury & Winchester, with Comments thereon', Société Jersiaise *Bulletin Annuel* 5, 251–65

Lee, G. (ed.) (1907) *Actes des États de l'Île de Guernesey*, vol. 2 1651–1780, Guernsey

Le Hérissier, R. (n.d., [1973]) *The Development of the Government of Jersey 1771–1972*, Jersey

Le Marchant, T. (1826) *Remarques et Animadversions, sur l'Approbation des Lois et Coustumier de Normandie usitées es jurisdictions de*

Guernezé et particulierement en la Cour Royale de la ditte isle (mid seventeenth-century), ed. J. Guille and P. le Cocq, 2 vols, Guernsey

Lenfestey, E. (1989) 'Legislative drafting in a mini-state', *Guernsey Law Journal* 7, 30–53

Lenfestey, J.H. (ed.) (1978) *List of Records in the Greffe, Guernsey, volume 2: documents under Bailiwick Seal*, London

Le Patourel, J. (1934) 'The Early History of St Peter Port', *Transactions of La Société Guernesiaise* 12, 171–208

Le Patourel, J. (1935) 'The Medieval Administration of Sark', *Transactions of La Société Guernesiaise* 12, 310–36

Le Patourel, J. (1937) *The Medieval Administration of the Channel Islands 1199–1399*, Oxford

Le Patourel, J. (1941) 'The Authorship of the *Grand Coutumier de Normandie*', *English Historical Review* 56, 292–300

Le Patourel, J. (1946) 'The Charters and Privileges, Laws and Customs of the Island of Guernsey', *The Bulletin of the Guernsey Society* 2, 3–8

Le Patourel, J. (1951) 'The Murder on Lihou Island in 1302', *The Quarterly Review of the Guernsey Society* 7, 3–6

Le Patourel, J. (1962) 'The Origins of the Channel Islands Legal System', *Solicitor Quarterly* 1, 198–210

Le Patourel, J. (1974) 'Guernsey, Jersey and their Environment in the Middle Ages', *Transactions of La Société Guernesiaise* 19, 435–61

Le Patourel, J. (1976) *The Norman Empire*, Oxford

Le Patourel, J. (1982) 'Le Monachisme Normand dans les Iles de la Manche pendant le Moyen-age', in L. Musset (ed.) *Aspects du Monachisme en Normandie (ive – xviiie siècles)*, Paris 109–114

Le Patourel, J. *et al.* (ed.) (1969) *List of Records in the Greffe, Guernsey, volume 1*, London

Le Quesne, C. (1856) *A Constitutional History of Jersey*, London

Le Quesne, G. (1992) *Jersey and Whitehall in the Mid-Nineteenth Century* (Third Joan Stevens Memorial Lecture), Jersey

Le Rendu, L. (1999) *The Positive Management of Dependency: Jersey's survival as a microstate in the modern world*, University of Oxford, D. Phil. thesis

Le Rouille, G. (1534) *Le Grant Coustumier du pays et duche de Normandie tres utile et proffitable a tous practiciens* ... , Paris

Le Verdier, P. (n.d.) 'Quelques notes biographiques sur Guillaume Terrien', in anon. (ed.), *A la Semaine de droit Normand: études communiqués par P. Le Verdier*, Rouen 21–28

Lightman, D. (1999) 'The Bailiffs of Jersey and Guernsey, the Lord Chancellor and the Separation of Powers', *Judicial Review*, 54–59

Lightman, D. (2000) 'The Jersey and Guernsey Bailiffs and the Lord Chancellor Revisited', *Judicial Review*, 111–113

Lord Chancellor's Department (2002) *A Guide to Government Business involving the Channel Islands and the Isle of Man*, www.lcd.gov.uk/constitution/crown/govguide.htm#part13, accessed 21 February 2003

Loveridge, J. (1974) 'The Constitution and Law of Guernsey', *Transactions of La Société Guernesiaise* 19, 393–415

MacCulloch, E., and Métivier, W. (1938) *A Report on the Nature and Extent of the Jurisdiction of the Royal Court of Guernsey over the Island of Alderney*, (1853), Guernsey

Maitland, F. (1908) *The Constitutional History of England*, Cambridge

Matthews, P. (2000) 'The Dog in the Night-time', *Jersey Law Review* 4, 164–68

McCammon, A. (1984) *Currencies of the Anglo-Norman Isles*, London

Morgan, J. (1997) 'Judicial Law Making in the Channel Islands', *Jersey Law Review* 1, 42–47

Musset, J. (1982) 'Formation et expression formelle de la coutume normande', *Connaissance de l'Eure* 46, 3–8

Nicolle, S. (1999) *The Origin and Development of Jersey Law: an outline guide*, revised edition, Jersey

Ogier, D. (1990) i 'The Authorship of Warburton's Treatise', *Transactions of La Société Guernesiaise* 22, 871–77

Ogier, D. (1990) ii 'The States of Guernsey in the Sixteenth Century', *Guernsey Law Journal* 10, 43–49

Ogier, D. (1996) *Reformation and Society in Guernsey*, Woodbridge and Rochester NY

Ogier, D. (2000) 'Chief Pleas Dinners', *Guernsey Law Journal* 28 (in press)

Owen, J. (2000) *Between Two Worlds: The British Perspective on Culture and Patriotism on the Channel Islands in the Long 18th Century*, Purdue University, PhD thesis

Ozanne, N. (1993) 'La Cour Ecclésiastique', *The Review of the Guernsey Society* 49, 104–09

Ozanne, N. (2002) 'The Faculty Jurisdiction of the Ecclesiastical Court of Guernsey', *The Review of the Guernsey Society* 58, 10–11

Packe, M. and Dreyfus, M. (1971) *The Alderney Story 1939–1949*, Alderney

Parks, E. (1992) *The Royal Guernsey Militia: a short history and list of officers*, Guernsey

Peyroux, E. (1970) 'Guernesey: evolution historique et condition juridique actuelle', thèse pour le Doctorat, Université de Paris, Faculté de Droit et des Sciences Economiques

Pissard, H. (1911) *La Clameur de Haro dans le Droit Normand*, Caen

Plender, R. (1998) 'The Rights of European Citizens in Jersey', *Jersey Law Review* 2, 220–42

Plender, R. (1999) 'The Channel Islands' position in International Law', *Jersey Law Review* 3, 136–57

Poirey, S. (1997) 'Le droit coutumier à l'épreuve du temps. L'application de la coutume de Normandie dans les îles anglo-normandes: le retrait lignager', *Revue Historique de Droit Français et Étranger* 75, 377–414

Pothier, R-J. (1821) *Traité des Successions* (1777), vol. 21 of *Œuvres complètes de Pothier. Nouvelle Édition*, Paris, 26 vols

Prison Board (1894) *Jersey Prison Board Case* papers, Privy Council, 10 vols inc. appendices, London

Privy Council (1946) *Evidence given before the Privy Council Committee on proposed reforms in the Channel Islands: Guernsey*, London (DB 26959/1)

Privy Council (1947) *Report of the Committee of the Privy Council on proposed reforms in the Channel Islands*, London (Cmd 7074)

Privy Council (1949) *Report of the Committee of the Privy Council on the Island of Alderney*, London (Cmd 7805)

Rait, R. (1937) 'Dicey, Albert Venn (1835–1922)' in Weaver, J. (ed.), *Dictionary of National Biography 1922–1930*, Oxford, 259–61

Ramsay, R. (2000) 'Will the Lord Chancellor's Position be Tenable in Future?', *Consilio* (6 May), http://www.spr-consilio.com/lordchance.pdf, accessed 5 April 2004.

Rippon, G. (1971) The text of a speech (also issued as an undated supplement to a *Billet d'État*) made to the legislatures of the Bailiwick of Guernsey, and a report of the following press conference, published under the respective headlines: 'Memorable day for the island' and

'Interference with island as tax haven impossible', *Guernsey Evening Press and Star* 19 November

Roberts-Wray, K. (1966) *Commonwealth and Colonial Law*, London

Robilliard, D. (1998) *Handbook for the Churchwardens of the Ancient Parishes of Guernsey*, Guernsey

Robilliard, St J. (1978) 'Tax Havens: the possible application of United Kingdom tax legislation to the Channel Islands', *The British Tax Review* 2, 111–17

Robilliard, St J. (1986) i 'United Kingdom in association with the British Crown: Bailiwick of Guernsey', in Blaustein, A. and Blaustein, P. (ed.), *Constitutions of Dependencies and Special Sovereignties*, Dobbs Ferry, New York, 1–74

Robilliard, St J. (1986) ii 'United Kingdom in association with the British Crown: Bailiwick of Jersey', in Blaustein, A. and Blaustein, P. (ed.), *Constitutions of Dependencies and Special Sovereignties*, Dobbs Ferry, New York, 1–91

Robilliard, St J. (1986) iii 'United Kingdom in association with the British Crown: Bailiwick of Guernsey: Alderney', in Blaustein, A. and Blaustein, P. (ed.), *Constitutions of Dependencies and Special Sovereignties*, Dobbs Ferry, New York, 1–39

Robilliard, St J. (1999) 'The Finance Industry: constitutional implications', *The Review of the Guernsey Society*, 55, 49–56

Round, J.H. (ed.) (1899) *Calendar of Documents preserved in France, illustrative of the history of Great Britain and Ireland, vol. i, A.D. 918–1206*, London

Routier, C. (1748) *Principes Généraux de Droit Civil et Coutumier de la Province de Normandie*, Rouen

Rowland, G. (2000) Appendix iv to Harwood, 2000, 'Responses of H.M. Procurer (*sic*) to questions raised by the panel', 113–27

Rowland, G. (2002) i A report of an interview by James Falla, under the headline: 'EU cynics think we help evasion', *The Guernsey Press and Star* 8 October

Rowland, G. (2002) ii 'Multilateral Policy Development and the Listing Process: balancing fairness and effective enforcement', in Commonwealth Secretariat, *The 2002 Commonwealth Secretariat Oxford Conference on the Changing Face of International Co-operation in Criminal Matters in the 21st Century*, London, 404–27

Sabine, G. (1948) *A History of Political Theory*, London

Sheridan, L. (1955) 'The Channel Islands', in G. Keeton and D. Lloyd (ed.), *The United Kingdom: the development of its laws and constitutions*, 1141–53

Sherwill, A. (1946) 'Judicial Reform', *Billet d'État* 17, 237–48

Sherwill, A. (1947) 'Some Notes as to the Origin and History of La Clameur de Haro and on its use in Guernsey in the Twentieth Century', *Transactions of La Société Guernesiaise* 14, 129–32

Société Jersiaise (ed.) (1877) *Extente des Iles de Jersey, Guernesey, Aurigny et Serk, suivie des inquisitions dans les iles de Jersey et Guernesey. 1274 – Edouard I*, Jersey

Stapleton, T. (ed.) (1840–44) *Magni Rotuli Scaccarii Normanniæ sub Regibus Angliæ*, 2 vols, London

Stevens Cox, G. (ed.) (1999) *St Peter Port 1680–1832: the history of an international entrepôt*, Woodbridge and Rochester NY

Stevens Cox, G. (ed.) (2003) 'My Dear Home Secretary: private letters from the Lieutenant-Governors of Guernsey to the Home Office, 1923–1937', *Les Iles de la Manche* 1, 28–33

Stevenson, W. (1975) 'England, France and the Channel Islands, 1204–1259', *Transactions of La Société Guernesiaise* 19, 569–76

Sunday Times (1999) Home Office advertisement: 'Lieutenant Governor of the Bailiwick of Guernsey', 21 November, sect. 7, 21

Sutton, A. (2002) 'Jersey and Europe: taking stock', *Jersey Law Review* 6, 165–202

Swinfen, D. (1975) 'The Daniel and Jersey Prison Board Cases of 1890 and 1894', Société Jersiaise *Bulletin Annuel* 21, 363–80

Tanner, J. (1930) *Tudor Constitutional Documents A.D. 1485–1603: with an historical commentary*, Cambridge

Tardif, E-J (ed.) (1881) *Coutumiers de Normandie. Textes Critiques: [Tome I] première partie: Le Très Ancien Coutumier de Normandie, texte Latin*, Rouen

Tardif, E-J (ed.) (1896) *Coutumiers de Normandie. Textes Critiques: Tome II, La Summa de Legibus Normannie in Curia Laicali*, Rouen and Paris

Tardif, E-J (ed.) (1903) *Coutumiers de Normandie. Textes Critiques: Tome I, deuxième partie: Le Très Ancien Coutumier de Normandie, textes Français et Normand*, Rouen and Paris

Terrien, G. (1574) *Commentaires du Droict Civil tant public que privé, observé au pays et Duché de Normandie*, Paris

Thornton, T. (2002) 'The English King's French Islands: Jersey and Guernsey in English Politics and Administration, 1485–1642', in G. Bernard and S. Gunn (eds), *Authority and Consent in Tudor England: Essays Presented to C.S.L. Davies*, Aldershot

Thornton, T. (2004) *The Charters of Guernsey*, Bognor Regis

Timbal, P-C. and Castaldo, A. (1990) *Histoire des Institutions Publiques et des Faits Sociaux*, Paris

Tramalier, T. (ed.) (1715) *Approbation des Loix, Coustume, et Usages de l'Isle de Guernezey, differentes du Coustumier de Normandie d'ancienneté observés en ladite Isle*, (1583), Guernsey

Tupper, F. (1876) *The History of Guernsey and its Bailiwick; with occasional notices of Jersey*, second edition, London

van Leuven, J.N. (1997) 'History and Practice of Parochial Taxation in Sark and Guernsey', *Guernsey Law Journal* 24, 111–22

van Leuven, J.N. (2004) 'Constitutional Relationships within the Bailiwick of Guernsey – Alderney', *Jersey Law Review* 8, 131–55

Venne, R., and Allez, G. (1992) *Alderney Annals*, Alderney

Vibert, R. *et al.* (1967) *Report and Recommendations of the Special Committee of the States of Jersey appointed to consult with Her Majesty's Government in the United Kingdom on all matters relating to the Government's application to join the European Economic Community*, Jersey

Vibert, R. (1991) *Memoirs of a Jerseyman*, Jersey

'Warburton, J' (1822) *A Treatise on the History, Laws and Customs of the Island of Guernsey*, Guernsey (from a late seventeenth-century manuscript. For its attribution to Christopher, Viscount Hatton, see Ogier, 1990 i)

Wheare, K. (1966) *Modern Constitutions*, second edition, Oxford

Williams, D.T. (1928) 'The Importance of the Channel Islands in British Relation with the Continent during the Thirteenth and Fourteenth Centuries', Société Jersiaise *Bulletin Annuel* 11, 1–89